Get Rooted, Stay Grounded &

THRIVE

Your Guide to Radical Personal Exploration

Janet Mary Cobb

Published by
WJRC Press
Chicago, IL 60641

Cobb, Janet Mary
Get Rooted, Stay Grounded & THRIVE

ISBN: 978-1-7362275-1-0
LCCN: 2022905123

Book design by Sabeer Al-shareef at www.donkaesuah.com

Dedication

To every woman who has struggled to find your voice, to commit to your own well-being, to choose joy, and to awaken your consciousness—that you may recover, uncover, and discover that which makes you whole.

Acknowledgments

The difficulty of writing an acknowledgment when completing any work is that I always feel the need to include everyone I've ever known. Truth be told, this book would not be possible without each person who has crossed my path. Not to mention, when I begin to thank those who have had the most direct impact on this project, I am more than likely going to forget someone. My apologies in advance.

I would be remiss if I didn't thank my husband, Willie, who always encourages me to work on and complete the projects I'm passionate about.

I'd also like to thank the many who have helped this project see the light of day:

- Andrea Holthouser, Kathy Kessenich, and Rachel Rajmattan who have been cheerleaders for everything that I say, write, or present to the public.

- Linda Berendsen who, years ago, read my poetry and created beautiful watercolors to accompany them.

- My son Trey, for helping envision the cover art. My son Wilson, who agreed to allow one of his charcoal drawings to be included (see Exploration Studio 3). My daughter Janalie for agreeing to her dance photo being used (see Exploration Studio 4).

- Those in my midlife blogging and Medium.com writing communities who have liked, commented on, and clapped for various pieces and parts of this compilation as they've been posted through the years.

- My WESOS (Women Entrepreneurs Secrets of Success) Sisters who introduced me to new artists and songs that replaced several of my long-held favorites in the Move with Music section.

- Yellowbridge.com where I cross-checked my Chinese language word parts to ensure that I wasn't completely mistaken in my understanding of the characters I've shared in each Challenge Your Perspective section.

- Stephanie Klein, editor and Professional Organizer at Sunshine Organizing Studio (www.SunshineOrganizing.com), who coached my developmental process and kept me on track in developing and organizing my manuscript to the very end.

- Victoria Hyla Maldonado, editor and author (www.victoriajhyla.com), who graciously and professionally line-edited my manuscript.

- All my early readers—Paula Andretich Davis and those who only you know who you are. Thank you for your honest reviews and your willingness to support my effort to bring *Get Rooted, Stay Grounded & Thrive* to life.

Table of Contents

Introduction

Get Rooted, Stay Grounded & THRIVE is designed as a guide for YOU to recover, uncover, and discover your next—your next iteration, your next step, your next turn, your next dream.

Notice that I'm carefully avoiding any language that implies a sense of improvement or trying to fix you. You may be feeling stuck in your current reality or searching for a different way to interact with your world. You may have had experiences that hurt you or you may be in a stage of transition. I am not trying to fix or change you. I offer this guide to support and empower you.

You see, I've never been a fan of popular platitudes like "If you can dream it, you can do it" and "You can be whatever you want to be." Point of fact: As a 5'2" woman, I can dream and believe all I want, but I will never be an NBA superstar.

Don't get me wrong. I believe in dreaming and hope. I believe in a desire to do something or be someone different than we are right now if we are not happy or well. We must hold a vision for the future filled with hope. We must dream BIG for the world we want to inhabit and the life we want to live.

I also believe that our dreams must be rooted. Not necessarily rooted in our current reality but in the reality of who we are, how we see ourselves, why we do what we do, what we want our lives to look like, and how we interact with the world around us.

How <u>I Got Here</u>, Writing <u>This</u> Book

Each of us has a story—experiences and moments, twists and turns, and sometimes a specific, inciting incident, all of which have influenced and shaped us.

This book came out of my story, and I share parts of it here, but it is not meant to be about me. I do not intend this book to be a vehicle to talk about myself; it is meant to be a vehicle for your own self-discovery. While I do present bits and pieces of my life experiences, I do so to offer questions, thoughts, and perspectives, with the hope that they encourage you to reflect on your own story. Ultimately, this book is meant to be about you.

During my half-century of life, I've encountered challenges and opportunities, experienced success and failure. I've tossed my life like salad a few times—turning it all upside-down, regrouping, starting over. I have had several careers and professional iterations: professional cook, teacher, librarian, fundraiser, and school administrator. I'm now a 58-years-young wife, mother to three young-adult children, and an independent author, speaker, consultant, and nonprofit strategy and personal development coach.

For many years, I dove in—all in—rather impetuously, and made my biggest life decisions without too much forethought. I spent years allowing others' attitudes, ideas, dreams, and demands to dictate my actions and reactions. In many ways, I was simply attempting to survive. Discovering that I had a voice and a choice to create the life I desired took time.

From the moment my father abandoned my mother when I was seven, leaving her to raise eight children alone, I had three life goals: to ride a horse, to see snow, and to visit Chicago. Raised on welfare in the government housing projects of a small, rural California town, my dreams were simple.

Professionally, I wanted to "be a teacher when I grew up," then I wanted to own a bakery or food truck, and then I hoped to become a high school counselor. I also had a profound belief that I would die young, which complicated any attempts to plan for my future. I never really believed I could or would grow up to be anything.

In February 1982, six months after high school graduation, I entered a convent to become a Catholic sister (nun). I was a young, rebellious class clown who had, just two years earlier, almost died from alcohol poisoning, abruptly entering a convent with the intention to profess vows of lifelong poverty, chastity, and obedience.

I spent thirteen years in the convent, seven of them living in Taiwan and Hong Kong, learning the Chinese language and culture, graduating from university as a Master Teacher, studying theology, and spending hours attempting to heal my inner child. I explored twelve-step philosophies, practiced TaiChi and Reiki, observed the horrors of Tiananmen Square and two Gulf Wars, witnessed life and death, supped with beggars and dined with bishops—and learned that the father who'd abandoned us had since created a "happily-ever-after" for himself and his new family.

At 30, I began to realize that while occasionally one word, one action, or one unexpected event can trigger major life changes, more often than not, it is a series of seemingly inconsequential conversations, minor decisions, and intangible vibes that converge in the center of the soul to create irreversible, irreconcilable shifts. Very slowly and then all at once, current reality becomes unbearable and your life, along with the illusions that created it, dissolves and you are required to begin again.

Much like gold tried and refined by fire, the moments we are called to start over may melt us, but as the impurities burn away, we are made stronger and more beautiful through the process. We just don't know it at the time.

These days, I refer to myself as a practical visionary. I consider myself a Taoist Christian Agnostic—a walking contradiction, a universal humanist wishing to embrace the fullness of all possibility in the universe.

While my background is rooted in Christianity, my spirituality embraces much more. My language and my values are flavored by my history. I agree with the teachings found in the four gospels—love your neighbor as yourself; be a good Samaritan; feed the hungry, clothe the naked, visit the sick. Part of my personal mission statement comes from Hebrew Scriptures—act justly, love mercy, walk humbly. I've also come to realize the universal nature of these truths, which can be recognized in numerous other religions, ideologies, practices, and cultures.

I resonate with The Tao, as I've come to know and understand it. I open myself to the idea of an ultimate source in the universe and of living in harmony, going with the flow, action without acting, and accepting the yin (light) and yang (darkness) in life.

In the pastoral ministry of my younger years, in my two-plus decades as a teacher, in my work leading retreats, and as a coach to women across the country, I've heard countless stories and witnessed the struggle of young and old alike to find their voice, embrace well-being, and choose a life of joy. This book is a compilation of writings and reflections, poetry and song that stem from my encounters with humans attempting to find meaning and purpose.

You will find a few references in this book to God and Christianity, but the language is circumstantial, flavored by my history, and not meant to be dogmatic. I hope you can access and resonate with the concepts underneath. Whether you find your source of empowerment, wholeness, and hope completely within yourself, in a community, or in God, Goddess, Higher Power, Universe, Spirit, Soul, Allah, Yahweh, Buddha, The Tao, the Divine, the Divine Feminine, or Grace—I invite you to embark on this journey with an openness to recovering, uncovering, and discovering all that makes you YOU.

About the Title: Rooted and Grounded

The root is where the life of any plant, vegetation, or tree begins. In the same way, our roots provide the nourishment, the context for where we begin. The root is what keeps us grounded.

For years, I lived in a toxic situation where I was constantly reminded to "bloom where I was planted." Cliché, I know, but it took me years to understand that sometimes we cannot bloom and blossom under our current conditions. We must imagine other possibilities to find the environment that will allow us to thrive.

If we never imagine what is possible beyond our current reality, we will be forever stuck. If we don't reach for new light, new soil, and new life-giving nutrients, we will shrivel, shrink, and cease to be the gift we are meant to be to the world.

In some cases, we may even begin to believe that we have no gifts to offer—that we don't deserve to thrive. Nothing could be farther from the truth.

About the Subtitle: Your Guide to Radical Personal Exploration

Each of these words has been carefully chosen to express my hope and intention with this work. You will notice that this is a *guide*, not a manual or a how-to. Nothing here is meant to tell you what to think or how to live. Like a tour guide, the thoughts expressed are to point out ideas you may never have considered and to offer points of interest for you to explore. Notice also that this is not **A** guide but **_YOUR_** guide. You get to decide. Follow your curiosity and your heart.

The word *radical* has gotten a bad rap, particularly in some contexts, but I challenge us, especially as women, to lay claim to the term.

We can think of a radical as one who dares to see things differently—the bold, brave individual who challenges the status quo. The radical is a revolutionary of sorts—and finding and following your own path can certainly lead to revolutionary changes.

Radical can also refer to the fundamental nature of someone or something. In nature, the radical is the stem or root of a plant. In music, the radical is the root of a chord. In mathematics, a radical is the root of a number. Linguistically, a radical is related to the root of a word.

As a synonym for the root, the radical is the point of origin, the nexus that holds something together, the source that gives it life.

By offering a "radical" approach, I invite you to return to the root, to recover your innate, inherent sense of self-worth. I invite you to uncover your strength, your courage, and your joy. I invite you to discover any gifts and talents that may be lying dormant.

I emphasize the word *personal* in the subtitle because I encourage you to make this all about you. You are unique. You will reflect, react, and respond to the various ideas presented throughout this book differently than any other person. Some points will resonate with you more than others. My stories may not be your stories, but I hope that by sharing them I embolden and empower you to reflect on your own.

You may find encouragement and strength in discussing your journey and experience with others. Fabulous! Remember, you get to do this YOUR way. I would offer a word of caution, however, that you do not allow how others respond to and interact with the process to confuse, silence, belittle, or discourage you. As you listen to others, allow yourself the space to incorporate their insights into your own process, but only to embrace them if they work for you.

By using the concept of *exploration*, I hope to ignite enthusiasm and excitement that leads to discovery. When we explore, we have no idea where it might take us or what we might find. Will these reflections lead to self-improvement? Maybe. Will you experience personal growth? Perhaps. Will it change you in some fashion? Doesn't every experience?

But more than anything, I hope you recover, uncover, and discover that which already lies within—and fully embrace who you are.

About the Book Structure

The goal at the center of this guide is to help you discover YOU, especially any parts that are currently lying dormant, untapped, unexplored, or unfulfilled. The process of self-discovery laid out here is rooted in reflection.

The book is broken into two parts: Part I will introduce a reflective practice, which I call *The Examen*; Part II will lay out a series of musings—thoughts that will facilitate your exploration as you apply the practice laid out in Part I.

The process I offer in Part I is meant to guide you through a positive encounter with your lived experience. Your experiences are what brought you to this current moment. Your actions and reactions may be holding you back. While my hope is that you realize a new iteration, understanding your actions and reactions is an important part of the process.

To that end, I have identified five facets of attentiveness, five distinct components which comprise a complete process of reflection. I have called these five phases "cycles."

I use the word *cycles* because steps and stages can lead us, mistakenly, to believe that the process is linear. In my experience, very little about personal discovery is linear.

We often circle back to face circumstances and lessons we thought we'd learned or outgrown. Or sometimes, as we move forward on our journey, we realize that in our eagerness to embrace the new, we've left behind something valuable.

These cycles are designed to root you in a practice so that as you recover dreams or desires, uncover truths, and discover new perspectives, you can return to them for further reflection.

These five cycles create an environment that will help you choose the life your heart and soul desire and deserve. As you reflect, you can envision who you want to be and what you want your life to look like. Then you can pursue the pathways that will get you there.

Part II is comprised of 26 sections, which I call *Exploration Studios*. The content of each studio is meant to be incorporated into your contemplative practice of reflection, your *examen*, and offer you opportunities to consider your perspective and perhaps trigger new ways to think about how you interact with yourself, others, and the world.

These are intentionally named "exploration studios" to resist, or outrightly reject, the notion that they are exercises or workshops. Like art, dance, and music studios, they offer opportunities to create. They give you room to play with your views, beliefs, and perspectives. The photos, reflections, questions, songs, and poems are not offered to judge you or trigger you but to give you a safe and sacred space to ponder.

How to Use the Cycles and Studios

As I've stated, this is YOUR Guide, and there is no right or wrong way to utilize it.

You may be a work-straight-through-let's-get-this-done type. Great! You can tackle one studio a day as you practice the examen, without cycling back, and you can conquer this quest in 26 days or fewer. If you prefer to take your time, reflect, and ponder, you may stay in one studio for a few hours, days, or weeks—however short or long you'd like.

If you are more tangential in your thinking, have little or no attention span, or never want to do anything in order—you're in luck. You can approach this content in bits and pieces. No matter where you open a page in this book you will find a morsel to munch on.

For those of you who are driven by a desire to do your best, by perfectionism, or by a fear of failure—take a direct shot through these cycles, start at the end or in the middle, or circle back again and again. You get to decide what it means to be successful in this endeavor. You can't fail or do it wrong.

You can move through these at your own pace and in any order you'd like. They are meant as a guide for you to recover, uncover, and discover You!

Do it your way!

Part I: The Examen

We begin by creating a space for an examen. Note the use of the word *examen* instead of the word *examine*.

To examine is to inspect or test. This word will likely conjure up feelings connected to a school examination or a medical exam. Our knowledge and skills were tested and graded. We passed, we failed, or we landed somewhere in between. We were perfect if we got an A and less than perfect with any other grade. Straight As may have been expected.

We may have experience of a physical exam at the doctor's office when we are sick, in pain, or when something is wrong. We may have an annual check-up to ensure everything is alright.

If you were raised Catholic, as a child you may have been taught to do the "examination of conscience" before going to confession. We compared and judged ourselves against a list of sins. We may have considered a list of virtues to decide whether we lived up to them, and if not, we knew we failed. Following this examination, we were responsible to recite our sins and ask for forgiveness. More often than not, we came up as not good enough.

The *examen* is meant to be a gentle review, a revisitation of experiences to notice how the spirit, our higher power, our goddess moves in our lives.

The word *examen* is rooted in the Catholic, Jesuit tradition of reflecting on your experiences in the spirit of gratitude. I learned of the *examen* during my years in a Catholic convent between 1982 and 1994. These practices were developed by St. Ignatius of Loyola, a Catholic priest who developed the practice of the examen, but it need not be a religious one. An internet search will reveal numerous popular and scholarly variations of the concept.

Through my own years of reflecting on my experiences and exploring new possibilities, as well as supporting others in their transformational journeys, I've adapted this examen as an approach for reflecting on our lived experience, a contemplative practice, if you will, which need not be tied strictly to any religious practice.

We simply reflect on our interactions, conversations, feelings, and responses. We pay attention, without judgment, in gratitude for how goodness, positivity, light, and love is present in our experiences. We may decide to "examen" our morning during a lunch break, our afternoon before transitioning from work mode to after work, and our evening before falling asleep.

This reflection is about more than just remembering; it is the process of being attentive to your emotions during your experience. We review our experiences from the perspective of how we envision ourselves and our lives. We look upon our current reality to see how it is different from what we envision. We pay attention to the moments and movements of our lives.

As you observe, you will discover new insights emerging, explore new possibilities, and let go of ideas, beliefs, and feelings which no longer serve you. As you let go, you will also have an opportunity to embrace new and different perspectives and ways of encountering yourself, others, and your world.

The steps to the examen, as I've adapted them, are simple.

1. Quiet yourself and recognize you are in a safe, sacred space, on holy ground as you sit with yourself. Feel free to invite your high power, the spirit, the Universe, God or Goddess to join you

2. Express gratitude, and with gratitude, review your day to be aware of the gift of the people, the experiences, and the encounters.

3. Watch your emotions. How did you feel in each "scene"? How did places, people, things, and activities make you feel?

4. If you notice feelings or moments in which your emotions were negative, consider what message those emotions are sending? Did you act or respond in a way that doesn't align with your vision of yourself?

5. Make note of one aspect or instance that you'd like to focus on. You might notice a moment of joy or gratitude or something you'd like to change or need to apologize for. Do you want to do more or less of something? Would you like to manifest something new? Do you need to let go of something old?

6. Look forward to later in the day or tomorrow. Notice the feelings that arise as you think about what is ahead. Do you feel fear, doubt, or frustration? Or excitement, joy, and eager anticipation?

Cycle 1: Envision

From the moment parents, teachers, and even total strangers asked us what we wanted to be when we grew up, we began putting ourselves in boxes. As we went through school and navigated family relationships and friendships, we were slapped with labels: not good at math, class clown, bossy, perfectionist, jock, teacher's pet, flighty, hothead, lazy.

These may not be your labels and boxes, but with a little thought, you can identify yours. Notice that so many boxes and labels are negative in nature.

We rarely consider adjectives like *hard worker, great cook, real athlete, business-minded,* and *true leader* to be boxes and labels, but sometimes even these adjectives can box us in and create unrealistic expectations.

Do your boxes and labels empower you or limit you? Have you allowed others' ideas to dictate your reality? Do you need a complete overhaul to find a new you? Are you looking for a new perspective? Do you fundamentally like who you are and hope to reflect and rejuvenate? Are you looking for a different way to clarify and express your values? Do you want to become even more YOU?

How Do You Envision?

The practice of creating vision boards to identify your dreams and life goals has taken many iterations over the years. From cutting and pasting pictures and words from magazines to fully digital creations, the methods to create and articulate your vision have evolved with technology.

Choosing a word or phrase of the year (WOTY) has also become popular. And with that come mottos, taglines, and questions of the year to help you stay focused, motivated, and moving in the direction you desire. The idea of personal branding has led many to formulate personal mission and vision statements.

What hasn't changed is the desire to envision a world and a future that does not yet exist and to focus on making progress towards it. Dreaming and wishing and hoping are part of our nature.

For many of us, academic success was defined by excelling at verbal/linguistic or logical/mathematical skills. For decades, the three Rs ruled in schools: **R**eading, w**R**iting, and a**R**ithmetic. This is a very narrow and limiting view, one that does not recognize or encourage other skills or types of intelligence. Traditional teaching methods, until recent decades, had little room for different types of learning styles for the auditory, visual, experiential, and kinesthetic learners. We may not have been encouraged to explore using other senses and approaches.

As a teacher, I often invited students to complete assignments based on multiple intelligences, a theory developed by Howard Gardner. Gardner introduced the idea that different people have different gifts and encounter the world differently based on natural tendencies and talents—and that education should incorporate more than just linguistic and mathematical means for transmitting and assessing knowledge. I developed lesson plans that allowed students to demonstrate their knowledge of a topic through song or dance, by painting or drawing, or through journal entries or class discussion. Those who preferred to take a quiz or write an essay certainly could, but this wasn't the expected assessment tool for every assignment.

Another example of the benefits of incorporating various intelligences into learning and self-discovery came during my many years as a retreat leader. I would often invite participants to use Play-Doh to represent their relationship to God as they understood God. For adults who likely hadn't molded Play-Doh in years, and who often relied on memorized or formulaic descriptions and definitions for God, the activity offered new perspectives and insight into themselves, their spirituality, and their next steps.

While the multiple intelligences theory has been discussed and developed, and some might even say debunked, through the years, I have witnessed children and adults engage with and come alive when offered content through these intelligences: nature, music, kinesthetic activity, spatial manipulation, interpersonal dialogue, and intrapersonal reflection.

The Exploration Studios, where you will apply the method of these cycles, are designed to incorporate and invite various aspects of these intelligences for your consideration. (More about this in Part II.) Perhaps approaching what you want your life to look like from the perspective of various intelligences will enable you to envision a life you've never allowed yourself to dream of before. When you set out to envision your next phase, your new iteration, and your best you, focus also on finding a language that speaks to your soul, whether it be art, music, nature, movement, etc.

Remember, these are not mutually exclusive nor are they exhaustive. What feels right in one moment or on one day may not work at another time. Don't be afraid to dip and delve into an avenue you've never had an opportunity to explore. **Be curious. Be silly. Be bold.**

Cycle 2: Evaluate

After you've spent some time practicing the daily examen filled with gratitude for your life, and have envisioned new possibilities, you are ready to evaluate your situation based on what you've noticed.

- What areas of your life might need to change so you can move from your current reality to your vision?

- What emotions arise most often? Are they positive or negative?

- Do you have patterns that repeat? Do you appreciate these patterns as empowering, or would you rather establish new ones?

- Do certain activities or habits keep you from being the person you want to be?

As we ask ourselves why we do what we do, we begin to get answers. Sometimes scary ones. You don't need to evaluate and make all the decisions at once. Face fears and temptations honestly. Take little steps. Divide and conquer. Pick one to focus on and then circle back.

During this process, spend time with people who support you as you articulate the good, the bad, and the ugly of your current reality. Surround yourself with folks who want to see you succeed.

Most of all, be gentle with yourself and remember that any words, actions, or attitudes that don't fit your vision do not define you. You have the power within yourself to think, speak, and act differently—when you are ready.

Cycle 3: Expel

Realizing that our current reality is not what we'd like our future reality to be isn't always easy. Neither is facing the "why" of it all—the reasons behind that disconnect.

But it doesn't have to hurt.

Once we've begun to understand, without judgment or blame, how we got to where we are, we can begin to politely invite the obstacles getting in our way to exit our lives.

The undesirable attitudes and habits that we now recognize are not serving us existed for a reason. Perhaps they were there to protect us or maybe to make us stronger. Maybe they're there because we held beliefs about ourselves, the world, or the universe that aligned with these actions at one time but not anymore. Now they are obstacles to creating the future reality we desire. Expelling those obstacles requires confronting the why of their existence when it rears its ugly head.

Let's recognize them. Let's thank them with gratitude and allow them to move on. Graciously invite them to leave, then let them go.

When you practice your regular examen, choose one area of focus at a time. How will you eradicate the thing that is holding you back?

For example, I recognized that staying up too late was getting in my way!

I had to ask myself, "*Why* was I staying up so late?" I've always considered myself a night owl. I got my best work and writing done in the wee hours of the morning. While this may be true, I had to ask whether it was an excuse. If I can only work on my novel in the middle of the night, then progress will be slow, but it isn't my fault. I can only stay up late so many nights.

See how this works?

Of course, nothing is wrong with being a night owl and writing into the wee hours of the morning, but it wasn't working for me anymore. I wasn't making progress on something that was very important to me.

So, I asked myself, "Is it really true?" What is it about the middle of the night that is so special? Could it be that when my children were little, the only time I was certain to be uninterrupted was while they slept? But these days, why have I made a habit of watching TV for hours until everyone has gone to bed before I even begin to write?

If I seriously want to complete the novel I've been writing for 10 years, perhaps I can test my firmly held belief. What if I shift my writing to early morning? What if, instead of trying to

---

function on 4–5 hours of sleep, I go to bed early, wake up early, and write when my brain is not fried, before a full day's work? I may not be able to do this all at once. But can I try? Will it work just as well?

By asking *Why?* and *What if?* we can release old habits and limiting beliefs without judgment and feel empowered to move forward.

Cycle 4: Explore

As we invite the attitudes, patterns, and practices that aren't working for us to exit the building, it is important to replace them with new thoughts, actions, and habits. Otherwise, the old will creep right back in. We can't leave an empty void. We must begin by exploring new possibilities. Will every new idea or experiment resonate? Probably not. But we can't be sure until we try.

Enter Part II. Now that you understand the *examen* and the method of reflection laid out in the 5 Reflection Cycles, it's time to apply them in a context designed to help you explore: the Exploration Studios. All 26 studios have been designed to help you find what works for you. Hopefully, you will find new thoughts, beliefs, dreams, habits, and desires—ones that better fit the future reality you've begun to envision for yourself.

Cycle 5: Embrace

Give it a little time.

As you ponder and reflect on your life and move through the studios, you may begin to feel things shift. You've lived with your beliefs, your patterns, and your practices for a very long time. Undoing them will be uncomfortable. You may feel a little lost. Repeating an affirmation like, "I choose joy" can feel very strange. Turning on loud music and dancing around your living room might leave you feeling silly or awkward. You might even think you're being fake or phony.

Don't be afraid to reach outside your comfort zone. Stretch yourself. Dip your toes in to test the waters. Dare to be different.

As you examen your day, ask yourself questions to help you evaluate your actions and reactions, expel what doesn't work for you, and envision what's next. Do the photos, words, ideas, and questions energize you? Do you feel uplifted? Do you want to embrace them and integrate them into your life? If not, you can let them go, too. Not everything you experiment with will work. That's okay.

You are discovering what gives you life, what fills you with joy, and what energizes and mobilizes you to create the life you desire. As long as you aren't hurting yourself or another, there is no right or wrong way to do life. Just do YOU.

When you are ready, embrace what brings joy, peace, and hope. Embrace that which makes you feel whole. Embrace the new YOU.

PART II: Exploration Studios

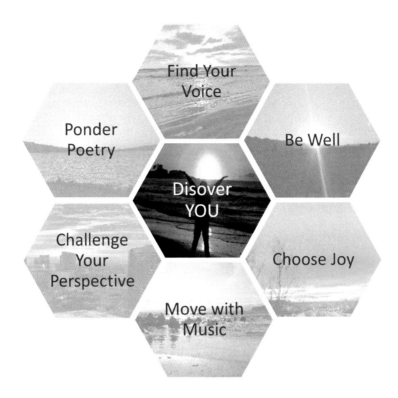

The Exploration Studios work hand-in-hand with your reflection practice. Each of the 26 studios presents seven opportunities for reflection and integration. You may review all seven in one day to soak in everything from that studio at once, or you may contemplate one opportunity each day, let your thoughts percolate, and experiment with new ways to approach your experiences.

1: Photo
Each photo (except for three that are noted) are pictures of nature taken by me. Sit with the photograph. How does it make you feel emotionally? Can you sense the temperature, texture, taste, or smell? Does it bring back any memories from your own life? How does it speak to you? Do you have opportunities to explore nature? Do you ever stop to enjoy the beauty around you? Can you take a picture to capture your thoughts and feelings?

2: Find Your Voice
Finding our voice isn't simply about having the courage to stick up for ourselves and say what we need to say. We may not even know what it is we WANT to say. Perhaps we've spent so much of our lives listening to and meeting the demands and needs of others that we've lost our ability to articulate our thoughts, beliefs, and desires. As you ponder the words presented in this section, ask yourself how they resonate with you.

3: Be Well
To be well is not just to be without disease. To be well is to embrace your whole self—body, mind, and spirit. Consider the words offered and the approach presented. Do you give more attention to one aspect of well-being than another?

4: Choose Joy

Each *Choose Joy* section offers a quote for you to ponder. Many of the quotes are from famous spiritual teachers, others from individuals unknown to the public. As you read the quote, what is your reaction? Do you accept the premise? Does it resonate? Do you agree or disagree with my thoughts on the quote?

5: Move with Music

The song title and artist name are offered. In the digital version of this guide, the song title is linked to the Official YouTube video. Take time to listen to it. Find the lyrics to ponder. Can you relate? Does the song make you feel empowered? Emboldened? Strong? Does it make you sad, or stir up longing? Whatever reaction you have is valid. How does it move you? Do you want to dance? If so, go for it!

6: Challenge Your Perspective

In this section, you will find a series of reflections connected to written Chinese characters. You don't need to know Chinese to benefit from these.

I share them because learning to read and write Mandarin and Cantonese in my 20s while living in Taiwan and Hong Kong, had a huge impact on my personal growth and worldview.
Language is a way for humans to interact and connect. Learning a language other than your native tongue and exploring how another culture uses language can be a mind-altering experience that sometimes shifts our perspectives, too.

In my daily language lessons in Taiwan, I learned that characters, which appeared to be a random and nonsensical set of lines to my untrained eye, consisted of word parts that often provide meaning and/or phonetic clues. No Romanized alphabet existed for native speakers, but each word could be identified in a dictionary according to a root, or radical, and the number of additional strokes it contained. Some radicals and word parts carry specific meanings while others do not. Not surprisingly, many emotional words include one of two versions of the radical for the heart: 心 or 忄.

I have done my best in these pages to offer an accurate description of the word parts, but my interpretations are rooted in how learning these words caused a shift in my perspective on life; it is not my purpose here to offer the historical etymology of each word. I share them with the hope that these words will open new thought patterns for you as well. May your radical personal exploration begin at the center of your heart—the root that holds the process together—and bring you personal insight and transformation.

7: Ponder Poetry

Poems can speak to the soul in ways that cut through the formality of prose. The rhythm, rhyme, and word choice are designed to express emotion and insight. Several poems feature the beautiful watercolor art of my friend Linda Berendsen—her artistic response to the words I shared. Try reading the poem aloud. Does it speak to you? Can you create a response? Does it spark, in you, a rhythm and rhyme? A dance? An image? An action?

Exploration Studio 1: Begin

Sunrise in Rye, New Hampshire

Find Your Voice

ASK.

As someone who had struggled most of my life to identify and articulate my own wants and needs, I hoped to instill in my children the authority to acknowledge and articulate theirs.

To encourage this, I would ask them to request rather than announce or whine. In other words, instead of just saying that they were hungry, I encouraged them to ask me to make food—and even more specifically, to cook them a specific food.

I wonder how different our lives might be if we taught children to identify and articulate their needs and desires instead of force-feeding them food, activities, school subjects, and assignments. How different might we be as adults in this world?

Learning to articulate our needs or desires and to ask when we need help doesn't mean we will always get our way, but it will help us find our voice and know what it is we're pursuing.

Be Well

ASK.

Body: When we begin a wellness routine, we usually think about getting active and eating right. We make plans, set goals, and jump in with our whole hearts and good intentions.

But have we stopped to ask our body what's doable? Do you ask:

- What makes you feel good? What do you need—from food, from activity, from rest?

- Why are you craving this food? How is this food making you feel? Is this food energizing you? Which foods give you energy?

- What are you capable of? What will make you feel good? How far can you be pushed? Do you enjoy this exercise? Would you prefer another?

- Do you get enough rest? Do you need something different—a new pillow, mattress, room? Do you need anything to help you get more rest—less TV, less computer time, more exercise, different exercise,more or less alcohol or sugar?

Mind: Wellness for our minds is about staying curious and challenging assumptions.

Ask questions about the world. Why are things this way? Dig deeper. How did we get here? How does this process or system really work? Ask about science, mechanics, nature, and psychology. We have so much more to learn. Let's become like the curious toddler who never stops asking "Why?" and "What's that?"

In a world where so many are stuck in their own opinions, and with political and religious divisiveness increasing rather than decreasing, do you try to listen to the other side? Do you hear the "why" behind others' beliefs?

I'm not suggesting that you compromise your principles. You have the right and obligation to live by your personal creeds. By challenging our assumptions, we can better own our beliefs with confidence and not feel threatened by someone else's point of view.

Asking "why" might help us keep our hubris and hatred, our anger and frustration in check. Intellectual understanding can perhaps lead to a compassionate response.

Spirit: In our attempts to be strong, we often hide our fears, feelings, frustrations, and even our dreams. We try to go it alone, not wanting to bother others or to appear weak. Sometimes we're afraid to ask our spirits, "What do you desire?"

A big part of caring for our spirits is to seek the support we need from those we love. Do you need to ask your family, friends, or even a stranger for help? Do you need to ask for space, alone time, or an assistant?

We cannot truly embrace self-care until we know what we desire from our lives, from our relationships, from our careers, and from our leisure. Don't judge, just ask.

Choose Joy

Joy is not dependent on circumstances; it is your own. It is not a titillation produced by things; it is a state of peace, of silence—a meditative state. It is spiritual.

Osho

I've always considered joy to be deeper than happiness. Joy runs deep—it doesn't mean we walk around like a smiling Pollyanna.

Joy resides deeper in the soul. Joy comes from the peace of knowing that we are MORE THAN our current circumstances and that we are not the sum of what might happen to or around us.

I don't know if this joy comes from (or leads to) acceptance of what is, but I do know that the moment I experience one, I also experience the other. And it may be in the moments I am forcing a smile because I'm having a "blah" day.

Move with Music

I Am Changing
Jennifer Hudson

Challenge Your Perspective

Are you angry?

怒

slave 奴 heart 心

One Chinese language character for *anger* is made up of the character for *slave* 奴 placed above the character for *heart* 心.

For years, I claimed I didn't care that my father had abandoned my mother with eight children when I was seven. "Don't know, don't care," I would say whenever an acquaintance would ask about him.

My apathy masked unimaginable pain and an anger that had taken hold of my heart. I began breaking rules, mistreating others, and refusing to believe I could be good at anything.

Years of self-doubt and self-punishment defined who I was, leaving me feeling unlovable and unworthy. I allowed others to put me down, manipulate me, and crush any dreams that I dared to dream.

I unconsciously fabricated a divine purpose for my pain. I spent years making reparations for my wrongdoings while I devoured books about healing the inner child and attempting to forgive my father and convince myself that I had made peace with being abandoned.

Moments of clarity through the years kept me from complete self-destruction. Ultimately, those moments cushioned my soul until I attended my father's funeral where anger boiled to the surface and forced me to admit my own reality.

Anger had enslaved my heart, making it impossible for me to love and believe in myself.

Anger can also arise throughout the day, any day. You might be ticked off at a driver who cuts in front of you or be bothered by the rudeness of a store clerk. You may rant to family and friends about how angry you are over some incident with your significant other, a friend, or even a total stranger.

Either way, you suffer if you allow your anger to keep a hold on your heart. Anger enslaves our hearts. We wallow in anger, punishing ourselves and those we love while the cause of our anger moves on, and the world continues to spin.

As you ask questions in this studio, ask yourself, *Am I angry?* Explore what comes up, what lies beneath, and the possibility of letting that anger go.

Ponder Poetry

Awaken

Delavan, WI, 6.29.1994

Little bird, do you know
The great potential within?
You can fly, you can soar
Reach heights never dreamt of before.
The songs in your heart
Will burst forth in harmony
Inviting all to sing the song
Of freedom and peace for which we long.
Your wings spread in flight
Catching swiftness in air
And the glitter from the sun
Lightening hearts of everyone.
Fear not, little bird.
To let yourself be taken
Into worlds of beauty above
Let your Spirit awaken, little dove.

Exploration Studio 2: Blossom

Lincoln Park Zoo, Chicago

Find Your Voice

BABBLE.

The word *babble* often has a negative connotation. We've all heard someone babble. They talk quickly and continuously, often excitedly, sometimes with no clear purpose, and are frequently misunderstood.

We babble when we can't find our voice, when we are unsure and unsettled, or when we are concerned that no one wants to hear what we have to say.

I'd like to suggest that if we doubt our ability to speak up or struggle to say what we really mean, perhaps we NEED to babble. Babbling is better than silence. When we babble, we remind ourselves and others that we are trying, that we exist, that we need to be heard.

Yes, ideally, we are all calm, centered, and totally attuned to the divine within us that drives us to speak our truth, *but in reality, we struggle.*

And perhaps instead of ignoring those who babble, we might listen to what they are trying to say beneath and behind their babble. Perhaps the one who babbles is screaming for a lifeline—to be heard, understood, to get help in finding and articulating their own truth.

Until we can declare our truth, let's babble and listen to others babble.

We might just find a kernel of truth somewhere in the frenzy.

Be Well

BRUSH.

Body: Brush your hair and your skin.

I'd imagine for most of us, brushing (or combing) our hair is a daily routine.

I'm not one to care much about how my hair looks. I've worn a wash-and-wear style my entire life (save the three years when I colored my hair, believing I needed to as a school administrator). I am a "seldom get a haircut" gal but when I'm feeling scruffy or out of sorts during my day, a good brush of my hair feels great.

When I was 28 and living in Hong Kong, my body began to fall apart. After several visits to the European doctor, I made a visit to a natural medicine doctor. Among many detoxifying tools, the doctor recommended one very simple one: skin brushing. *Is brushing your skin a thing?*

The skin is one of the major systems the body uses to rid itself of toxins. His remedy was for me to use a natural bristle brush and, beginning with my feet, move in small circles up each leg and over my entire body before showering. This stimulates circulation and opens the follicles to release toxins as you shower.

Mind: Brush up on a talent or skill you've let go.

In 1993, when I returned from seven years of living in Asia, I was thinking and dreaming in Cantonese. I sometimes forgot how to say certain words and phrases in English. On the phone, I was proficient enough that when I spoke Mandarin, many people thought I'd been raised speaking Cantonese and vice versa.

Recently, as I completed an online professional profile, one of the questions asked if I had "fluency in any of the following languages," and the list included Mandarin or Cantonese. I couldn't click the box. I was disappointed. I've lost what, at one point in my life, was very important to me! I've been itching to brush up on my language skills.

Do you have a skill that used to be important to you that you've let go? Will it do you good to refresh it?

Spirit: Brush away negative thoughts.

Negative thoughts can wreak havoc on your well-being. We cannot completely control the thoughts that pop into our heads. We can, however, brush them away. We can become aware of the thought, thank it for any purpose it serves, and brush it along if it does not serve us. We don't need to fight them or beat ourselves up about them. Acknowledge them and brush them away with a positive thought, a prayer, or a routine that helps you move beyond the negativity and toward your deepest desire.

Choose Joy

Connect to your Joy: You will always be able to connect to your JOY when you make choices that are nourishing, supportive, feel expansive and uplifting, speak to your heart, and feed your soul!

Unknown

To make the choices that allow us to connect to our JOY, we must know what activities, foods, habits, and relationships nourish, support, expand, uplift, and feed our souls.

So many of us pay little attention to how our sleep patterns, the weather, the foods we eat, and what we drink impact us.

I sometimes stay up late watching a silly program and snacking too late. I sleep poorly and feel like I've been hit with a ton of bricks in the morning. Eating junk food at night (or too often at any time) is not nourishing for my body or my soul.

Getting sucked into my social media feeds, sitting too long in one place, and spending time with some family members saps my energy and drags down my soul.

We have the power to choose.

Let's choose what expands and uplifts us and speaks to our hearts!

Move with Music

Follow Your Arrow

Kacey Musgraves

Challenge Your Perspective

How busy are you?

heart 忄 death 亡

One day during a period of personal crisis before I returned from Hong Kong, the word *busy* 忙 struck me. The character contains the heart radical 忄 placed next to 亡, which means death. Simply put: heart + death = busy. This juxtaposition struck me profoundly.

Throughout my years in the convent, I'd been indoctrinated with quotes like, "Idle hands are the devil's workshop." I was encouraged to keep busy instead of thinking too much. Work became my constant source of distraction and a certain comfort zone whenever I became fragile, life became chaotic, or I was faced with a difficult decision. Keeping busy became my crutch to ignore the voice within me that cried for attention.

My experience was not unique to me. Many of us have been raised with a strong work ethic, to give 110%, to pride ourselves on being busy. The very way we introduce ourselves and get to know others is rooted in what we do for a living—not in what brings us joy.

Don't get me wrong. We all have responsibilities that we cannot neglect. We must make a living, pay our bills, and feed our families. In meeting our daily obligations, we create a sense of purpose. We wear a badge of honor announcing to the world that we are capable and responsible and that we can handle life.

We are all busy. We're so busy that stores, gas stations, fitness centers, and restaurants are open 24 hours. Our coffee makers and ovens have time delays. We text, email, or FaceTime—while driving, schlepping children, or waiting in line. Our children have 20 minutes for school lunch, to cram in the required minutes for each subject—to pass the test, get into the best schools, and climb the metaphorical ladder to success.

Yet, our very busyness is often what keeps us from enjoying our family and friends. Our busyness leads to frustration, stress, or rude and short-tempered attitudes. Is our busyness bringing us closer to the ones we love or driving us farther apart?

Being still calms the chaos and forces us to face the void at the center of our souls. Is busyness the cause of our pain or an excuse to avoid facing our own emptiness? Has keeping busy resulted in the slow death of our heart, and physical and emotional exhaustion? Or did having a dying heart drive us to stay busy and develop workaholic tendencies?

To avoid the ache, the fear, and the uneasiness that settled—perhaps long ago in childhood, perhaps from mistakes made later along the way—do we create reasons for not living out our hearts' desires whether spoken or unspoken, admitted or not? Are we afraid of the quiet and stillness? Do we keep busy to avoid the pain?

Ponder Poetry

Daybreak

A moment
Alarm rings
Hit snooze

A moment
Ring
Hit snooze
A moment

A moment
As energy
drains
With each reach
For just a moment
Of comfort
Safety
Sanity?

A moment
Alone
Without
Judgment
Vulnerability
Responsibility

A moment
Alone with
A heart heavy
And the burden
of knowing
Failure
Depression
A moment
Defeat
Isolation
Depression

A moment
To muster the smile
The how are you
Of casual conversation

A moment
To formulate
Your answer:
Great
Good
Fine
OK
Hanging in

A moment
To convince yourself
That someone cares
That you matter

A moment
To rise
to the challenge
Of one more
Moment

Exploration Studio 3: Nurture

Photo credit: Charcoal drawing by Wilson Cobb

Find Your Voice

CRY.

Someone once told me that crying shows a lack of faith in God. I didn't know enough at the time to speak up. Instead, I attempted to hold back my tears, to offer them up, and to be strong.

Instead of honoring the emotions (sadness, fear, anger) that triggered the tears, I swallowed them, as best I could, and apologized when they spilled out.

For years, I didn't realize how unhealthy stifling emotions can be. With time, I learned that, to find peace, be content, and share joy, I first needed to find my voice.

Sometimes we must shout from the mountain tops. Sometimes we share quietly with a friend. Sometimes the only voice we can muster is the silence of a tear.

Be Well

CELEBRATE.

Often when we focus on self-care, we think about what we haven't done or "should" do. We make "do this, don't do that" lists.

An important part of being well is learning how to CELEBRATE.

Body: Celebrate your body.

Celebrate the good and the less than perfect; what works great and what hurts or causes pain; what you love and what you wish was different. Celebrate the body that has brought you to this day.

Mind: Celebrate your mind.

Celebrate when you are quick and alert and when you feel like you're in a fog. Celebrate the things you remember and the things you forget.

Spirit: Celebrate your spirit.

Celebrate your up moods and your down moods. Pay attention to how you feel. Don't judge, just honor. Honor each and every emotion. Allow yourself to feel. Pay attention to how you feel. Celebrate all the feels.

I do not want to be flippant. I want to honor the reality that some of us live with challenges, like depression or anxiety, that are difficult to manage. I believe that while living with these issues, it is possible to honor and celebrate the wonderful person you are in any small way that you can.

Celebrate all that you have; all that you are in body, mind, and spirit; and all that you already do to be well.

Choose Joy

Even a rainy day can't dampen our joy.

Unknown

When the sun is shining, I feel a bounce in my step and enthusiasm in my soul. I embrace a sunny day with the confidence to conquer the world.

Not so much on a cloudy, gloomy—what Winnie the Pooh would call blustery—day unless my agenda includes snuggling up with a good book. My funk is instantaneous.

But, remembering that JOY is a choice, I try with all my might to find joy in the dreary. I drag myself out of bed and onto the porch to stare at the clouds, hoping for an "a-ha" moment.

Clouds just hang there blocking the sun, not raining. "Get on with it," I think.

Then I'm reminded of a t-shirt I once bought for my son that read, "I'm not lazy. I'm overflowing with potential energy."

I have always honored procrastination, recognizing the need for ideas and energies to percolate—in me and in others.

So, now I try to welcome gloomy days as reminders of potential and possibility. With potential and possibility, we find joy.

Move with Music
Girl Can't Be Herself

Alicia Keys

Challenge Your Perspective

Are you charitable?

heart 忄 blood 血

One day as my companion and I traveled by public bus along a mountainous route in Taiwan, we ran into a traffic jam.

When we learned that an accident had caused injuries to several people in the cars ahead, one young man suggested that we disembark so the bus we were on could be used to transport the injured. The passengers on the bus exited, single file, with little more than a mumble.

As we waited in the 90-degree heat, some passengers pulled out umbrellas to shade themselves against the sun; others sat on their haunches on the roadside, fanning themselves with whatever they had at hand. The bus went ahead without us as cars moved aside to let it pass. There was no whining or groaning about the inconvenience; the disturbance was no greater than if we had all been standing in line at the grocery store.

I was moved by their charity.

We often reduce the word *charity* to the donation of money or tangible items. We "give to charity." But doesn't charity mean so much more?

The Chinese character for *charity* is made up of *heart* 忄 and *blood* 血. In this light, charity assumes the giving of your heart's blood, the life-giving force running through your veins.

When someone is bothering us, charity demands that we be patient. When someone is rude, charity dictates that we be kind.

If charity is understood to be the giving of money or tangible items to the less fortunate, then charity is simply taking pity on another and giving them something material, external.

In the famous passage that begins "Love is patient" from 1 Corinthians 13 in the Christian Bible, we are reminded that charity is patient, kind, never boastful, and never puts on airs.

How much more this charity means than simply offering financial assistance to the needy, no matter how great. How much more charity means when it costs us our energy, a piece of our heart,

Ponder Poetry

I Cry

Chicago, 6.28.1994

I cry and cry for help.
Yet no one hears
through the laughter or sees
in the smile, the pain.
Will I ever know the place—
that niche where I may blossom,
the soil in which I'll thrive?
Instead, I push on:
getting things done,
accomplishing tasks given to me.
Inside the empty hollow
Yearns for fullness,
for connectedness,
meaning and purpose.
Am I running,
trying to dodge
the reality of my own emptiness?

Exploration Studio 4: Grow

Child dancing

Find Your Voice

DECIDE.

The day after Christmas 1994, two of my siblings and I drove from the San Francisco Bay Area to Las Vegas to meet our father, whom we hadn't seen in more than 20 years. We were in our mid-30s, at various stages of our own lives, each dealing with a variety of feelings related to the encounter.

About seven years old when he left home, I remembered very little of him. But that day, he said one thing that forever shifted my understanding of myself.

He said, "I remember you used to get so upset when you didn't get your way. And you'd say, 'I wanted to (insert desired activity), but nooooo,' because you had to follow the older kids."

As the seventh of eight children, growing up near the poverty line in the 1960s and '70s, not getting my way was common. But when my father shared this memory, I realized that somewhere along the way, I stifled my ability to express desire.

Running off to a convent at 18 and spending the next 13 years allowing someone else to make even my simplest decisions—like when to wake, eat, sleep, what to wear, watch, read, and even how to vote—hadn't encouraged my ability to identify my desires or make decisions for myself.

I'd left the convent just months before meeting my dad that day, but I realized then why it had taken so long for me to leave. This doesn't mean I always get my way now or that I don't throw the occasional fit when I don't, but I made it my personal mission to make my own decisions, find my voice and speak up. And I've made it my life mission to support others to do the same.

Be Well

DANCE.

As a tween and teen, I LOVED to dance. I could dance to all kinds of music, with all kinds of people, in all kinds of places. Dancing was part of me. I wasn't necessarily good at it, but I have basic rhythm. We did the Bump, the Hustle, the Slide. *Soul Train* and *American Bandstand* were favorites.

Then I entered the convent, and all dancing stopped.

After leaving the convent, it took a little while for me to feel totally comfortable, but I began to love dancing again. There's nothing like a night out on the dance floor. Then quickly, along came marriage and children, and dancing became more homebound.

When my children were little, I would hold dance parties in the living room. But, alas, my children didn't fall in love with dance (or roller skating or ice skating).

Now, I'm not one to go out dancing. I would rather avoid the expense and the drunken fools often found in clubs, etc.

But housecleaning happens twice as fast when I blare music throughout the house and sweep, scrub, and fold to the beat. I often grab two- or five-pound weights and an aerobic step, turn on my workout playlist, and dance around the room with no set routine. Dance has become one of my go-to forms of exercise. I just follow how the music moves me.

Body: Dancing is exercise.

Dancing certainly burns calories and gets the heart pumping!

Mind: Dancing is mind-altering.

Dance relieves stress and helps you forget your troubles. Dancing produces proteins that spur new neuron growth and cell connections, making our minds more supple.

On top of that, when you return to your problems, you'll likely have a fresh take and new ideas for dealing with them.

Spirit: Dancing increases happiness and sparks empathy, and releases endorphins, which produces a high.

Did you also know that dancing promotes empathy? Even just watching someone else dance can make the same neurons fire as if we're dancing ourselves.

Choose Joy

Joy is a decision, a really brave one, about how you are going to respond to life.

Wess Stafford

When all is well personally, interpersonally, socially, and politically, when babies are smiling and the sun is shining, finding joy is easy.

When times are tough, deciding to be grateful and to choose JOY takes a bit more. At these moments, we smile and fake it 'til we make it. We hope. We decide to look for the positive and to hold on through the darkness.

In times of tension, when we are stressed and distressed, we MUST decide how we respond to life.

Deciding to choose joy gives us the strength and courage to keep going through the tough times.

Move with Music
Brave

Sara Bareilles

Challenge Your Perspective

Are you careful?

小心

small or little 小 heart 心

Be careful. A common expression.

When our children are learning to do new things like walk, climb, run, and play ball, we advise them to be careful.

In Chinese, this expression is made up of the word for *small* 小 and the word for *heart* 心. To be careful is to use a little heart.

For much of my time in the convent, I was considered clumsy and admonished to "be careful." One of my Chinese nicknames was even Da Ben Jiang, which translates as "Big Clumsy Elephant," (usually spoken with affection). I was continually admonished to be careful. I tried to be careful, but with time, my caution became restrictive.

If we become too careful, we run the risk of becoming small-hearted. We close ourselves off to new experiences and adventures. We avoid risk. We are afraid to fail. The temptation is to become so careful, so meticulous, and so attentive to detail that our heart becomes small.

In the days I was known for my clumsiness, I claimed a carefree attitude as my excuse.

I eventually came to understand that I was not so much carefree as I was careless. My carelessness was an unconscious creation of reasons for others to be angry with or disappointed in me. That way I had an excuse for them to reject me.

As I learned to love and value myself, I no longer needed excuses, and I could put a little heart into everything I did.

Finding balance between using a little heart in our words and actions so as not to bring harm to ourselves or others and becoming so careful that our heart shrinks is no easy task.

But learning not to be careless, when to be careful, and allowing ourselves to be carefree opens us to new possibility and promise.

Ponder Poetry

The Front Porch

A simple concept
For years communities
watching, sharing, visiting.
With the nod of a head,
the wave from across the way,
those close, enjoying one another's company.
Today gates, alarms, and hectic schedules
leave no time for the porch.
Instead, we post, comment, like, share, tweet, and retweet.
The world has become our front porch
As we search for connectedness, meaning,
A moment for our voices to be heard,
And our life to be shared.
Social media.
Our 21st-century front porch.

Exploration Studio 5: Prosper

Lake Michigan, Chicago

Find Your Voice

EXPRESS.

Finding your voice does not always mean that you need to speak words.

Self-expression can come in many forms:

- The clothes you wear, your shoes, your hairstyle, piercings, and tattoos.
- Your home decor, your car, the neighborhood where you live, and the shops you frequent.
- How you budget and spend your money.
- Who you befriend and how you spend your time.

Issues arise for us when our forms of expression don't align with our inner values.

Articulating our values, our philosophy, and our purpose is the first step to expressing who and how we want to be in the world—and then creating a life to match.

Be Well

EXHALE.

Have you ever been attentive to how you breathe? When you breathe do your shoulders move up and down? Does your stomach expand and contract? Does your chest move slightly? How many breaths do you take a minute?

Have you ever watched a baby breathe while they sleep? If you watch a baby sleep, you'll notice that as they breathe, their stomachs expand and subtract.

Body: When you breathe in through your nose and out through your mouth, your gut will expand with each inhale and retract with each exhale.

Deep breathing in this way helps the shoulder, stomach, and back muscles relax. You'll notice improved digestion, decreased cravings and emotional eating, and increased lung capacity when exercising.

Mind: Taking long, deep, slow breaths also slow the mind. If you've practiced Yoga or TaiChi or meditation in general, you know that breathing is important to the meditative process. By slowing our breathing, we slow our minds.

We can enter what Deepak Chopra refers to as "slipping into the gap" that helps us recognize our deepest desires and detach from them so the universe can take care of the rest. We can more readily let go and live in the present.

Spirit: If you've ever hyperventilated or experienced a panic attack, you've experienced the benefit that slow breathing has on your emotional state.

Deep, slow breathing also can help us deeply feel our emotions. By slowing our breaths and feeling our emotions, we are less prone to judging them as "good" or "bad" and more able to accept them for what they are: feelings.

We get to decide how we will honor and respond.

Our thoughts and feelings do not control us. They do, however, offer us the gift of insight. When we slow our breathing and take a moment to exhale, we can listen to the secrets our body, mind, and spirit hold for us—about who we are, what we desire, and how we want to "be" in the world.

In practice, being constantly alert to our breathing can be taxing, especially at the beginning. So, try to find moments to exhale when you're in line at the grocer, at a stoplight, on hold over the telephone, or for a few minutes before eating.

Choose Joy

Comparison is the thief of joy.

Theodore Roosevelt

Comparing ourselves, our lives, our belongings, and our gifts to others robs us of joy because someone will always have more or be better than us.

Comparing is the root of all misery, right? Maybe not.

Let me explain....

Comparing can be a motivating factor: "If he/she/it/they can have it or do it, maybe, just maybe, I can, too."

This doesn't mean I lose my joy. My joy isn't outside of myself but resides within me—in acceptance of what is and in hope of what is yet to come.

Rather than comparing myself to someone who is living the life I want (whether it be physical, emotional, financial, social, or spiritual) and putting myself down because I am not yet there, I can compare my dreams to my reality and know that more, different, better is POSSIBLE.

Like most anything else in life, it is not the comparing that robs me of joy but what I do with, or how I respond to, the comparison.

So today I invite you to compare and carry on.

Move with Music
<u>Most Girls</u>
Hailee Seinfeld

Challenge Your Perspective

Do you envy others?

忌

oneself 己 heart 心

Have you ever felt envy?

When I was a young sister preparing to be sent out on mission, one of the other young sisters was being sent to Taiwan.

She'd had the desire in her heart for many years to serve in China. She'd studied Chinese in school and read extensively about the culture and customs. She had prepared.

I just wanted to go because everyone was so excited about her going. She was getting all the attention. I was being asked to serve in Oregon. No one really cared. I began to feel ignored.

The more I thought about it, the more desperately I wanted to go to Taiwan.

In Chinese, the word for *envy* is formed by placing *oneself* 己 above the *heart* 心.

I couldn't rejoice in her joy. I couldn't even rejoice in what was being asked of me because I had put my ego above love.

When we become the center of our own heart, it makes it very difficult to move beyond envy to seek good for, and in, other people.

Envy gets at the root cause of this insatiable desire to have what belongs to another. Envy convinces us that we are more deserving or more important than someone else.

Envy causes us to be cruel to others. Driven by envy, we sacrifice honesty, friendship, and integrity in our quest for the object of our obsession.

We may not admit, or even recognize, envy as it takes control of our hearts. But each time we are unable to rejoice for someone's good fortune or we criticize the success of another, we make ourselves the center of our own hearts and allow envy to reside in the recesses of our souls.

Ponder Poetry

Why?

Why do you do what you do?
Why, they ask, again & again.
I used to know.
When the gospel was my why.
What would Jesus do?
Feed the hungry
Clothe the naked
House the homeless
Instruct the ignorant
Let little children come to me
Be that person of integrity, honesty, kindness.
Act justly. Love mercifully.
Walk humbly.
This was my why.

Why I taught in Catholic schools
Why I gave 200%
Why I never made enough money!

But now I see, money is not evil.

Money allows me to
feed the hungry,
clothe the naked,
house the homeless,
instruct the ignorant,
and let the little children
be who they are meant to be.

From abundance
From a place of peace
From all that I AM meant to be
This is why I am who I am
And why I do what I do.

Exploration Studio 6: Rise

Cactus Flower

Find Your Voice

FORGIVE.

You've likely heard the expression "forgive and forget." I've never agreed with it. By conflating the acts of forgiving and forgetting, we have pulverized the act of genuine forgiveness.

Yes, we can forget about the man who cuts us off in traffic and let go of the snub of the casual acquaintance. Trivial hurts require simple fixes. Forget about them.

But true emotional pain, which can only be inflicted by one we have trusted or loved, demands forgiveness. When we experience disrespect, deceit, and betrayal, the pain cannot be brushed away and easily forgotten. It will eat away at us, causing emotional and physical unease (even disease) and return to haunt us.

In moments of genuine hurt, we must forgive—and, I dare say, never forget. To forgive is to find our voice.

Forgetting, on the other hand, leaves room for the person to repeat the behavior that caused the pain. When we forget about the pain, we make room for the person to do it again because we've forgotten all about it. Forgetting takes no courage. Forgetting does not lead to growth or salvation or healing.

Forgiveness brings true freedom. In acknowledging and articulating the pain, we say, "I forgive you." With these words, we offer love, peace, hope and joy, not because we have forgotten but because we have forgiven. Every time we remember the pain, we forgive again. Each time we repeat, "I forgive you," our voice becomes stronger. Until we have truly forgiven, we are limited in our ability to give again, to love, to act upon our hearts' desires.

Be Well

FAST.

Have you ever fasted? For weight loss or health, religion, or clarity of mind?

Fasting is more than a fitness fad. Fasting as a practice has been around for centuries.

Fasting comes in a wide variety of shapes and sizes. Some folks abstain from all foods, others from only certain foods. Some tout the benefits of long-term fasts, others believe in intermittent fasting, which entails establishing rhythms for eating on specific hourly or daily cycles. Some fast purely for body fitness, others for purity of the soul.

Because I'm neither a doctor/health practitioner nor a saint, I'll fast from providing the details of HOW to fast and simply share thoughts on how fasting might impact body, mind, and spirit.

Disclaimer: I am not a medical doctor. I've not been trained in any natural or alternative medicine theory. I share what I've read and what I know from experience. If you are thinking of undertaking any fasting regiment, please do your own research and consult a doctor or practitioner of your choosing to give you the go-ahead.

Body: Fasting may help:

- Sync circadian rhythms and fight off metabolic diseases.
- Keep the weight off in the long term, without restricting calories.
- Lower your risk for cardiovascular disease.
- Slow down the aging process.

Mind: Fasting:

- Removes and eliminates damaged molecules and cellular waste that could lead to neurological diseases.
- Increases a protein that prevents the death of stressed neurons, which could lead to cognitive disorders like dementia and Alzheimer's.
- Creates new connections in the brain and improves cognitive function.

Spirit: People fast:

- To focus on spiritual matters and enhance concentration during meditation.
- To aid in yogic feats like generating inner heat and raising vibration levels.
- To control fleshly desires or resist gluttony or as penance or atonement.
- In solidarity with the poor and to counterbalance modern consumerism.
- To advance a political or social-justice agenda.

Choose Joy

Today is the perfect day to be joyful.

Janet Cobb

Why not?

What constitutes a perfect day to be joyful?

Isn't today as good a day as any or even THE perfect day to be joyful?

Accepting all that today holds, whether we like it or not, will lead us to joy.

Remember that joy is not giddiness.

Joy comes from believing and trusting in what was, what is, and what is yet to be.

Today is the only day we have. We are not promised another.

What are you waiting for?

Move with Music
Rise Up
Andra Day

Challenge Your Perspective

Do you need to forgive?

寬恕

wide, relax 寬 excuse 恕

One phrase in Chinese for the word *forgiveness* is the character that means *wide* 寬 and the word that means *excuse* 恕.

To widely excuse.

Perhaps this means that we must offer as many explanations and perspectives as we can for the reason someone caused us pain. To me, this means that we attempt to excuse their actions because we don't know their motivation, we don't know their pain, and we've never walked in their shoes.

As we reflected earlier, forgiving and forgetting are not the same things. We must forgive over and over again.

In the Christian Bible, Jesus said to forgive "seventy times seven." Does this mean we allow someone to hurt and wrong us 490 times? Or rather, could it mean that each time we remember the pain, we forgive again, perhaps until we lose count?

But what does it mean to widely excuse?

To excuse doesn't mean that we let them do it again. It means we don't hold a grudge or get revenge. To excuse doesn't mean we forget the wrong done to us. If we forget, forgiveness is not necessary.

With forgiveness, we acknowledge the hurt and refuse to allow it to harden our hearts. We remember the wrong and offer peace and goodwill to the one who hurt us. And we move on.

Ponder Poetry

Caterpillar

Los Gatos, Summer 1993, during a 30-day silent retreat

The caterpillar crawls along the blade of grass unseen
Much like the searching soul: unsure of where it's been.
Unknown to self, not seen by human eye
The caterpillar and the soul will surely have to die.
They enter into solemn space and unsoiled holy ground.
In quiet stillness, the true self can be found.
With courage, they weave a sheltering cocoon.
And deep inside the heart of love, alone, they find room.
The room to let the treasure, hidden deep within their soul
Transform what once seemed useless waste
into nuggets of pure gold.
And slowly, if they wait to create and to reveal
The pain and fear that dying held gently start to heal.
And from the tomb of darkness, caterpillar and soul have spun
New life, more precious than ever dreamt, has already begun.
The caterpillar turned butterfly
flutters aloft each gentle breeze
The soul, inflamed with love, falls into God's arms with ease.
What's ahead for butterfly and for the soul set free
doesn't frighten.
They both proclaim:
I am finally free!

Exploration Studio 7: Illuminate

Lincoln Park Zoo, Chicago

Find Your Voice

GRUMBLE.

To grumble is to complain or mutter about something under your breath or in a muted manner.

Grumbling implies that few, if any, hear our complaint. Grumbling implies that we have no solution and no intention to act in the manner needed to address the problem about which we are complaining. When we grumble, we need not take responsibility for the dissatisfaction we are feeling. We don't have to confront the cause of the dissatisfaction.

But does grumbling serve any purpose in our efforts to find our voice? Does grumbling bring joy to us or to others? Or is grumbling an exercise in futility?

I'd like to suggest that grumbling holds immense potential and power.

Like the gibbering of an infant, grumbling can be a moment of hope—hope that we will find just the right words to express our desires, hope that others might understand us some day.
And like the first fruit fly in the kitchen, grumbling reminds us that something needs our attention and ignoring it will only make it worse.

And like the first daffodils of spring, grumbling reminds us that what lies dormant through winter brings beauty and joy in the spring.

Grumbling holds the immense power of promise that one day we will have the strength to not only face (and mutter) our dissatisfaction but the courage to meet it head on and perhaps find others who will accompany us along the way.

Grumbling can be the kernel of personal transformation and even powerful social movements—if only we pay attention.

Be Well

GINGER.

You may have noticed that every word in this Be Well series is a verb. Becoming well and employing self-care involves action. So, when you read the word *ginger*, think "to ginger."

To ginger can mean, literally, to add ginger (root, spice, powder, juice) to flavor a dish, but beyond its aromatic, wonderful flavor, ginger has many health benefits.

My personal favorite remedy when I'm feeling a cold or flu coming on is to boil chopped up ginger root and green onion in a sweet liquid like cola or water with maple syrup, molasses, or honey. It's simple but effective. Drinking this concoction under the blankets after a hot shower knocks out all the germs.

And a chunk of crystalized ginger settles most upset stomachs and heartburn.

But "to ginger" can also mean to invigorate or liven up a person or a conversation.

Body: When you ginger your food, your body will thank you. Ginger is known to:

- Reduce nausea and gas.
- Improve gut health—reducing stomach ulcers, ulcerative colitis, and Crohn's disease and treating diarrhea.
- Promote sweating, which detoxifies the body and helps treat the cold and flu.
- Fight inflammation—reducing muscle pain and arthritic symptoms.
- Prevent menstrual cramps.
- Lower LDL cholesterol.
- Improve insulin resistance and control diabetes.
- Alleviate inflammatory skin conditions.
- Prevent infection.
- Boost metabolism.
- Reduce risk of breast and colon cancers.
- Relieve asthma.

Mind: In addition to the peace of mind you get when you physically feel better, when you ginger your food, you reduce the risk of dementia and Alzheimer's and improve cognition.

Not to mention, when you ginger a conversation, you can elevate the discourse and challenge your mind.

Spirit: Last, but not least, ginger is an aphrodisiac, which might enliven your spirit.

Choose Joy

*Sometimes your joy is the source of your smile,
but sometimes your smile can be the source of your joy.*
Thich Nat Hanh

Some days we wake up feeling "blah" or even downright sad and on the verge of tears for no real reason. I know I do.

My life is good. I count my blessings. But smiling on days like that can be a struggle.

Smiling through these feelings helps us find and share joy with others perhaps because it forces us out of our own negativity.

I am not suggesting that we ignore our emotions or smile to please other people.

I am not trying to be flippant about serious mental health issues.

I am not encouraging anyone to ignore the reality of toxic or dangerous situations "with a smile."

But on those days when you wake up on the wrong side of the bed, perhaps a smile can bring you and others joy.

Move with Music
Pocketful of Sunshine
Natasha Bedingfield

Challenge Your Perspective

Have you ever faced disaster?

災

river 巛 fire 火

From the moment I learned that the Chinese word for *disaster* is made up of the words *river* 巛 and *fire* 火, I was struck by the inherent contradiction between what is necessary for life and what destroys it.

Water and fire—two such necessary gifts without which we could not sustain life, and yet both are so powerful and destructive. Rivers swell and flood their banks, destroying lives. Islands are completely ravaged by hurricanes, tsunamis, and floods, and California burns with wildfires.

Too much or too little of good, necessary things, including our emotions, can wreak havoc and cause destruction.

When we allow ourselves to view minor inconveniences or temporary setbacks as disasters, and let our emotions get the best of us, we unknowingly could be opening ourselves to destruction or blocking life-giving possibilities.

Let's welcome the minor floods and small fires that come our way so we might better prepare ourselves to face true disaster if it strikes for ourselves or others.

Ponder Poetry

Potholes and Blessings

Astute drivers navigate
around the tire-damaging sinkholes.
Potholes abound.
With each change of weather,
a new hole appears.
Tires roll down bumpy roads.
Rocks ding the bottom side of the car.
Potholes: a reality of life.

We know.
We slow down, swerve around, avoid the worst roads.
Drive accordingly: roll along at attention. Be careful.

Like potholes, troubles come:
From unexpected job loss, medical expense,
Unanticipated car repair. Life happens.
In recession, we slow down
Avoid extra bills, save—just in case.

A child's classmate loses her mother to cancer—
a year after losing her father.
A brother loses his second wife. Twice widowed.
Hundreds, if not thousands
Lose their homes to tornadoes, fires, floods.
The list goes on.
And everyone has a story.

A transient man stands on the corner,
A sense of calm respect,
Asking passersby for a SMILE.

Amid life's potholes, we count our blessings and smile.

Exploration Studio 8: Bloom

Mary Catherine McKay Arnold
(January 8, 1932-March 17, 2018)

Find Your Voice

HONOR.

My sister began her beautiful reflection on our mother with the statement: "Our mother was not perfect."

These words epitomize the meaning of HONOR.

To truly HONOR someone, we must speak the truth with love, respect, forgiveness, and admiration. Our mother's imperfections are part and parcel of her tremendous strength, courage, and ability to love.

The same holds true when we consider how we, as individuals, find our voice. Before all else, we must embrace our reality—as imperfect as it may be—and honor the person we have become.

My mother, with her imperfections, was a woman who found her voice through trials and tribulations regardless of what anyone else thought and was never afraid to be herself in the world.

We must honor ourselves and others despite, or perhaps because of, our imperfections.

Be Well

HUG.

I wasn't raised to be much of a hugger.

My family didn't hug much, but this doesn't mean we didn't love each other. Our love and affection were demonstrated differently—primarily through sarcasm and service. For me, a perfectly placed sarcastic remark from one of my siblings releases the same dose of serotonin as a physical hug.

Plenty of evidence exists to show that hugging increases serotonin and lowers blood pressure, making it good for the body, mind, and spirit.

But rather than thinking about what a hug does for us, I'd like to think about what we offer to others with a hug.

I like to think of a HUG as an offering of:

> **H**onest
> **U**nabashed
> **G**ratitude

Body: Do we hug with our whole selves, unabashedly? Or are our hugs stilted and stiff?

Mind: Do we hug out of habit or obligation? Or do we hug because we honestly welcome this person with open arms?

Spirit: Do we hug in gratitude for the relationship we have with this person and for all they mean to us in our lives?

When you hug with your heart, your hands, your head, or a quick sarcastic remark with Honest Unabashed Gratitude, you create a moment of healing and well-being for a loved one, a friend, a tree, or yourself.

Choose Joy

*Sometimes we miss out on the bursts of joy
because we're too busy chasing down the extraordinary moments.*

Brené Brown

The word "extraordinary" strikes me as a word that can cause more pain than good.

If one thing or moment is extraordinary, everything else is "ordinary" and somehow "less than" or not important or special. Much like the word "normal," anything that is not the norm is considered deficient and wrong as in "abnormal."

Perhaps we would experience joy more often if, instead of constantly comparing and searching for something more, we allow ourselves to experience objects, events, and others in the glory of simple uniqueness.

Move with Music

Masterpiece

Jazmine Sullivan

Challenge Your Perspective

Do you have courage?

勇

path 甬 strength 力

During an outdoor education camp with my sixth-grade class years ago, I led them on a night walk through the woods. I explained that courage is acting as if you are not afraid even when you are and still moving forward.

At the time, I feared dogs and failure more than anything. My life was fairly simple. I lived in a convent. As I saw it, I had little use for real courage.

As I consider the Chinese word for *courage*, which combines the words for *path* 甬 and *strength* 力 , I ask myself if my concept of courage is too limiting.

When I think of courage as the path of strength, I see courage as something that grows with time.

Courage doesn't happen overnight.

My life imploded within weeks of encouraging my students to walk in the dark. I left the convent and tossed my life about like salad. I had to start over. I was 30.

Since then, I've faced real fear. Being in nonprogressive labor of our firstborn child and having to undergo an emergency cesarean section. Watching my new son spend a week in the neonatal intensive care unit. Watching my toddler daughter have seizures after a traumatic fall. Being jobless with three children. Raising biracial children in a violent, racist world.

These more challenging moments as well as everyday decisions give us the grace to face the life-changing moments of fear with courage.

As we face daily decisions about finances, health issues, schools for our children, political platforms, personal relationships, and our careers, we can find strength along the path.

We make the best decisions we can in the moment, drawing strength from our prior experience and the wisdom of those around us, in the face of uncertainty and forces beyond our control.

Ponder Poetry

Those I Miss

My home, reduced to an empty nest,
My children eagerly gone their way.
The hours of driving without a rest
Melted like snow on a summer's day.
I breathe in deeply, this kind of hush
My companion in apparent peace.
Gone the frenzy of a constant rush.
Hail, the chance to write my masterpiece.
Laptop, cozy fire, and warm tea set the stage
My long-imagined moment of bliss
Crumbles, not from fear of the blank page,
But from a soul coveting those I miss.

Exploration Studio 9: Imagine

Papago Park, Phoenix, Arizona

Find Your Voice

IMAGINE.

Imagine if you never worried about what others thought of you.

Imagine if you always said exactly what was on your mind, with respect and integrity.

Imagine if you truly heard the fears, hopes, and truth of others—and responded with compassion.

Imagine if you let go of "should" and embraced "could."

Imagine if you always did what you knew to be right and good for yourself and others.

Imagine if you honored your past, embraced your present, and anticipated your future.

And imagine if you, and every other person on Earth, did these things with gratitude for the unique gifts of every other person.

How would our world be different than it is right now if we worried less and imagined more?

Be Well

IMAGINE.

If we believe that all life is energy and vibration, and that our thoughts become our reality as many scientists, philosophers, and spiritual guides say, then our ability to imagine is one of the most powerful tools we possess to envision and bring about our deepest desires.

Body: Imagining takes a certain amount of relaxation, a release of tension, an out-of-body experience.

Mind: To imagine is to let the mind wonder. In a sense, aren't dreams a form of imagining on some level? And dreams happen when our bodies fall into REM sleep. REM sleep is the time when our minds process our experiences and rejuvenate. When we imagine, we aren't tied to our current reality but able to free our minds to explore possibility.

Spirit: When our bodies are relaxed and our minds are free, our spirits are lifted, expanded, and open to hope.

Ignatius of Loyola encouraged the use of the imagination in prayer to tap into deepest desires. Imagination is not always a simple flight of fancy. Instead, to imagine is to know that our current reality, as good or not so good as it is, isn't the entire story.

To imagine is to hope.

To imagine is to believe in the possibility of "Next?"

Choose Joy

Joy is portable—bring it with you.

Unknown

On the surface, it makes sense that we can carry joy with us and share it with others.

But the idea that joy is portable also challenges the common belief that we would be "happy *if only...*"—if only we had a different job, lived somewhere else, didn't have toxic people in our lives, if our bodies were stronger or healthier, and so on. It's the "grass is greener" concept.

But like the saying, " *Wherever you go, there you are,"* we can only bring joy with us if we embrace it, if we choose it.

Sometimes finding joy in the tough places gives us the courage and strength to begin the journey away from that which is harmful or holding us back.

If we can't find joy within us, we might need to ask if it is the situation that is robbing our joy or if it is our perspective. Because if we don't figure that out, our lack of joy will come with us wherever we go.

Move with Music
<u>You Gotta Be</u>

Des'ree

Challenge Your Perspective

What do you imagine?

想象

think 想 elephant 象

The Chinese words for *imagine* make me chuckle. Think of an elephant. I have no idea why the character for elephant was chosen to depict the word imagine (or whether imagine was used to identify the word for elephant). But when I learned the word, I was reminded of the old saying, "How do you eat an elephant? One bite at a time."

We can't imagine eating an entire elephant, so when faced with the idea, the only way to approach it is to begin with one bite.

The same holds true for our big, bold goals, dreams, and visions.

When we are stuck in our current reality, perhaps feeling overwhelmed, the only way to move from where we are to where we want to be is one small bite at a time.

Much like Anne Lamott's story, which led to her book *Bird by Bird*, when her brother asked her father how he would ever complete a big school project on birds, her father simply replied, "Bird by bird."

Consider the quote attributed to Francis of Assisi, which says, "Start by doing what's necessary; then do what's possible; and suddenly you are doing the impossible."

And, if you can find the speech by Martin Luther King where he talks about your life's blueprint, take a listen. He speaks about the eternal principles of beauty, love, and justice and then says what has become a popular quotation, "If you can't fly, run. If you can't run then walk, if you can't walk, crawl, but by all means keep moving."

Ponder Poetry

One Day

Wisconsin, 10.29.1994

One day it happens; we don't know why
But all's confusion, and from our hearts we try
To find the self we've never known.
Because from pain, we called others' hopes our own.
We see the path we've walked along
We've read the story; we've sung the song.
But at once we know we've trod another's road.
We've carried the burden of someone else's load.
Although we struggled along as best we could
We know it's time to let go of shoulds.
Boldly, we set out on uncertain ground
To seek the way, 'til then, not found.
To boldly go, where no one's gone before
Seeking the key to unlock our treasure's door
Afraid to reach beneath layers of pain
We pull and tug, alas, in vain.
The tangled web while on our journey, we weaved,
Has twisted in knots as we struggled not to leave.
Yet deep inside we know it's true.
If we patiently ponder and look anew
We'll find the thread that brings us hope
Gently working through we learn to cope
It isn't necessary to frantically cling
Nor need we fret what each day brings
From deep within our hidden souls
The well springs forth to make us whole.
The hidden treasure buried years ago
Has been recovered; we come to know
The peace and joy the discovery brings
Is worth more than gold and diamond rings
The love and freedom each day gives
Confirms the belief, my Spirit lives.

Exploration Studio 10: Embrace

Freshly fallen snow, Rushville, Illinois

Find Your Voice

JUXTAPOSE.

"We hold these truths to be self-evident..." Don't worry, this is not politics. I borrow the phrase to invite us to consider the truths about ourselves that we hold to be self-evident, the things we believe so deeply that we never challenge them. Often, we don't even know they're there.

For years, I believed a number of things, none of which were true: I believed that my dad went crazy because I was born, that God wants me (and others) to suffer; I believed that my intelligence would be my downfall—all of these and many more untruths...

To stop allowing these various "truths" to control my life, I needed other options. I needed to juxtapose these beliefs with contradictory ones in order to chisel away at the negativity and degrading effects of the *un*truths I'd held to be self-evident. Contradictory statements can simply be opposites:

- My dad suffered from mental illness at the time I was born, not because I was born.

- My intelligence is a blessing, not a curse.

Or you can begin to juxtapose them with entirely new truths—affirmations like:

- I accept myself and all my experiences.

- I am free to share my gifts with the world as I choose.

Think about the mental tapes and messages you received, perhaps as a child, or the opinions others might have of you even today. Do they keep you from finding your voice, being content, and sharing joy with others?

Which words, phrases, or beliefs can you JUXTAPOSE to trigger new truths?

Be Well

JINK.

Jink is not a common word in my world, but when I looked up the definition, I knew it needed to be included in any discussion of being well.

The standard definition of the verb *jink* is "to change direction suddenly and nimbly, as when dodging a pursuer."

To BE WELL, we are sometimes called to nimbly and suddenly change direction: physically, mentally, and emotionally.

Body: When we aren't treating our bodies respectfully—jink.

Mind: When negative thoughts creep into our choice to live a positive, joy-filled life—jink.

Spirit: When what we feel hurts (like anger, sadness, grief, fear), AFTER we allow ourselves to HUG the feeling and imagine new possibilities—jink.

Choose Joy

Embrace Joy: Instead of embracing the misery that comes with the many problems we encounter every day, just find one memory that brought you joy and think on that. It's a good way to start building a positive attitude.
Kimberly Dawn (ScentofFaith.com)

My first choice would certainly be to arrange my life so as not to encounter many problems every day. When we experience autonomy, freedom, and minimal stress, joy tends to come more easily.

But many folks juggle concerns and burdens—health, family, finances—that make choosing joy more difficult. And for those dealing with their own or a loved one's depression, chronic illness, poverty, etc., the effort to choose joy is that much greater.

I believe, though, that a person's attitude impacts their mental and physical ability to face and deal with problems and be resilient. At the moments when we or someone we encounter seems stuck in their misery, perhaps it is an opportunity to offer them a share in our joy.

Many years ago, during one of the periods in which my life was being tossed about like salad, I landed in Chicago with little to my name and no idea how I'd reinvent myself.

I was walking home from the grocery store, my arms laden with bags and my soul laden with grief about the life I'd lost. I passed a man who appeared to be homeless asking passersby for change. When he looked at me, instead of asking for change, he simply said, "Oh sweetheart, is there anything I can do to help you?"

Something shifted in me at that moment. I can't say that my life immediately improved and all was well, but his kindness gave me new strength to carry on.

We might never know what a simple smile, a kind word, a small gesture like running an errand, completing a chore, or providing monetary support will mean for someone. More often than note, we don't know what another person is going through. But if we take advantage of opportunities to offer random acts of kindness, perhaps another might loosen their grip on misery and open their arms (and hearts) to joy.

Move with Music
Who Says
Selena Gomez

Challenge Your Perspective

Is jealousy eating at you?

妒忌心重

envy 妒忌 heart 心 heavy 重

As if envy isn't bad enough, the Chinese expression for *jealousy* implies that it happens when we envy until our heart is heavy.

We've all had moments of envy when we think, "I wish I had this, that, or the other," when we see someone else's good fortune and have that momentary flash: "Wouldn't that be nice?"

But an idiom for *jealousy* is to "eat vinegar." As one who does apple cider vinegar shots, I can tell you it isn't pleasant.

Jealousy can eat at you and turn your life sour, just like vinegar.

Envy and jealousy do nothing to lessen the good fortune of the other person; rather, the opposite is true. Unlike admiration, which acknowledges the blessings, talents, and gifts of others and uplifts you in the process, jealousy brings you down. Your own heart becomes heavy.

When envy and jealousy fester, we become consumed by what we lack and are unable to appreciate what we have.

When we find ourselves entertaining thoughts that begin with "I wish..." and "If only...," perhaps it is time to count our blessings, open (or begin) a gratitude journal, or write notes of appreciation to those we admire.

Ponder Poetry

Addiction

Chicago, 2009

Baby carrots. Crunchy,
sweet, beta-carotene.
Good for you. Good tasting.
I am addicted.
People chuckle.
"What a great thing!
Addicted to carrots."
A handful is healthy.
A pound, great.
Two pounds—a bit much.
Five pounds. Everyday.
Skin turning orange.
I am addicted.
Blueberries. Fresh. Frozen. Delicious.
Phyto something or other.
A handful. Detoxing.
A pint. They will mold.
A 2-pound plastic container.
Great tasting. Good for me.
Easy to snack. On sale.
Worth it. Brain food. I won't turn blue.
I am addicted
Chocolate. Work. Exercise.
TV. Religion. Carbs. Coffee.
Diet this or fat-free that.
Just a pick-me-up.
Can't function 'til I have it.
One glass. Need to relax.
Gotta keep fit.
No big deal.
Until it is a big deal.
And gets in the way of life.
I am addicted.
Invading the control centers of my brain.
Becoming the driving force
behind every movement and decision.
Flavoring life as it comes at me,
Helping me avoid, or cope, or deal.
Preventing me from creating
And living the deepest desires of my soul.
I am addicted.

Exploration Studio 11: Elevate

S'mores

Find Your Voice

KEEP ON.

A country song by Rodney Atkins encourages us to "keep on going" whenever we're going through hell. And not to show it if we're scared, because "You might get out before the devil even knows you're there."

Learning how to keep on going when things are tough is one of the most critical steps in finding your voice.

You likely developed family, friend, and even romantic relationships before you found your voice. As you work to speak up—to announce, babble, cry, decide, express, forgive, grumble, honor, and imagine—your family and friends might resist the changes you are making.

Transition is tough, but you can keep on keepin' on.

Be Well

KINDLE.

Some say it takes seven days to form a habit; others say 21. Developing a habit may take a bit of time, but in my experience, it takes no time at all for a habit to crash and burn.

As someone who has resisted routine, I've recently established a morning habit: 20 minutes each morning under a sun lamp listening to meditation music, drinking hot tea, and working on a jigsaw puzzle or coloring. I enjoy the calm, peaceful ritual to start my day.

When I dig into intense home repair or writing projects, I sometimes work late into the night, which throws off my morning ritual, as well as my sleeping, eating, and exercise patterns.

Getting back into the flow can take time, but I don't beat myself up about it. Instead, I focus on how I will kindle my physical well-being, energy, productivity, and joy.

"Kindle" is synonymous with verbs like spark, arouse, ignite, encourage, excite, activate, and pique.

Body: Physically, I try to be attentive to which forms of movement encourage even more movement.

Which sleep-eat-exercise patterns and habits make me feel alive and which drain me? What happens in my body when I eat too much, too late, or too little? While I can operate on virtually no sleep when I must, I ask—does this kindle joy and productivity? Is it more energizing to take long 5-mile walks at one time each day, or will it spark better self-care to break it up throughout the day?

Mind: When I face project deadlines or have many responsibilities, social media and cable news take a back seat to everything else.

And I've noticed that with less exposure to those outlets, I have more energy to handle the rest of life. I often use social media as an opportunity to zone out for 10 minutes, to refocus, and return to work ready for another hour or so of productivity. Evening news, which kindles an eagerness to make a difference in the world, has become redundant and deflating. What previously piqued my interest and lit a fire in me now saps my focus and frustrates my efforts to be productive.

And so, I remain attentive. I ask myself, "What kindles my curiosity, drives my productivity, encourages me to make a difference in the world?"

Spirit: While I can have the most physically fit body and the sharpest mind on Earth, the bottom line I keep asking is, "What kindles my joy and uplifts my spirit?"

Choose Joy

Press on—there is joy ahead.

Unknown

If today is tough, please believe.

Believe in yourself. Believe in possibility.

If you're feeling great today, remember that those you encounter may be struggling.

Believe you are being given the opportunity to offer them joy so they can press on.

Move with Music
Hold On
Wilson Phillips

Challenge Your Perspective

Are you kindhearted?

仁

person 人 two 二

Being kindhearted is one of the five virtues extolled in Confucianism because kindheartedness rids society of selfishness, jealousy, and hatred.

The word for kindhearted is simple: two persons. To be kindhearted is to recognize that we are in relationship with others. The person beside, across from, or in front of us requires our attention and deserves our respect.

Being kindhearted also reminds us that we are not alone. We must sometimes accept the assistance and support of another. We must treat ourselves with respect because our habits and decisions influence the lives of those around us.

Being kindhearted does not mean that we must save the world, win an award, or become a hero. Being kindhearted does not mean we personally cure all the world's ills.

Being kindhearted *does* mean we no longer look upon another human being, regardless of status, intelligence, beauty, or mental state as an "it," only important in the context of our own story, what we can see, or what they can do for us. Being kindhearted also means we accept the negativity, pain, and suffering of our existence and recognize that others, like us, are caught up in the limitations of our human condition.

This, to me, is why the word is so profound. This word, which simply depicts two persons, allows for a transcendent, even transformational relationship, beyond you and me. If we are kindhearted, we remember that we are all connected, and that the actions of one person impacts another. How profound is it to recognize a relationship between two people who might otherwise not be related?

It reminds me of the question posed to Jesus: "Who is my neighbor?" Jesus answers with the parable of the Good Samaritan in which a stranger, an outsider (someone who was considered "less than" in the society of the time), shows kindness to someone who has been injured.

Is our kindheartedness limited to those we know and love or those who agree with our religious or political beliefs? Or is every person, regardless of their perceived usefulness to me, worthy of dignity, respect, and kindness?

Ponder Poetry

Embracing Brokenness

Chicago, 6.5.1995

At the very core of my being,
in the darkness beneath
the pounding heart
and heaving chest
a tension rises,
a child
longing to be loved
a youngster striving to be free
a woman, searching for wholeness.
Games were played
Obsessions clung to struggles
And battles fought.
Still, fulfillment alludes.
Until I turn within
And find, in the darkness
Not an empty void
but, at the very core of my being
a loveable child
a carefree youth
and a woman embracing her brokenness
and becoming whole.

Exploration Studio 12: Sparkle

Dandelion pappi

Find Your Voice

LAUGH.

When I was a child, I often giggled uncontrollably, rolling on the floor until my sides hurt when someone tickled me. In grade school, children would chase me down to tickle me and watch me giggle. I became known as "Tiger" because I would bite them to protect myself. Although this recess activity faded, throughout middle school and high school, I was the class clown, offering jokes and laughter, usually at the teacher's expense.

My senior yearbook quote read, "Laugh and the class laughs with you, but you stay after school by yourself."

When our mother passed a few years ago, family members posted photos from years past. I was struck by the smiles, chuckles, and wide-mouthed laughter captured in the snapshot moments of our lives. I became a little more subdued in my convent days, but photos still captured moments of laughter and joy.

I remember laughing with my children when they were small, but then life got tough with the recession and job loss and financial struggles. I realized it had been a few years since I'd laughed heartily, let alone regularly. I don't remember the last time I giggled hysterically.

I'm not suggesting that laughing is the only measure of health and happiness. Laughter can often hide sorrow and pain. I used giggling, laughing, and telling jokes to avoid tough conversations. Rather than face a painful situation, we can simply crack a joke to lighten the mood. Sometimes this is needed, but is it always the best solution?

When we explore ways to be authentic and find our voice, we are called to pay attention to what might be lurking behind the laughter.

Be Well

LAUGH.

Laughing is critical to well-being.

Body: Laughing burns calories and massages intestinal muscles.

Mind: Laughing helps you forget your troubles, even if just for a little bit.

Spirit: Laughing sparks joy and dispels sadness.

Plus, laughing feels good!

Choose Joy

To get joy, we must give joy, and to keep joy, we must scatter joy.

John Templeton

The idea of scattering joy in this quote struck me and reminded me of the phrase "joy someone."

Several years ago in Chicago, a Christmastime billboard advertising the lottery read, "JOY SOMEONE."

I loved the phrase instantly. Given the trend of turning nouns into verbs, I thought, "What better word than JOY?"

To scatter is to disperse or spread something randomly. I think of the dill, the mint, and the pansies scattered throughout my garden, driving my neighbor crazy but making me smile.

Children seem to have a natural tendency to scatter joy. Somewhere along the way we lose that natural tendency to choose, give, and scatter joy.

Perhaps we need to be far more intentional in our efforts.

Move with Music
Firework

Katy Perry

Challenge Your Perspective

Are you loyal?

center 中 heart 心

To be loyal, one must hold the person, idea, or institution to which one is loyal in the center of one's heart. The word for loyal is the character for center 中 placed over the radical for heart 心.

The word reminds me of a definition for friendship I first heard in high school: "A friend is someone for whom you would accept full responsibility for their actions."

Only when we know someone and love someone well enough to say that we trust their decisions and actions as if they were our own, would we call someone a friend. Everyone else is an acquaintance.

While you may not agree with this definition of friendship, I think it speaks to loyalty. Loyalty implies trust.

How often have we been loyal to a job or an institution, sacrificing our personal time and energy, only to be disappointed that the loyalty wasn't returned?

And how often has someone we thought we knew surprised us by their words or actions?

Loyalty can be tough because we need to find balance and create harmony between being loyal and willing to trust AND setting our boundaries without closing ourselves off.

We can ask ourselves, for whom would I be willing to go to jail? For what would I be willing to die?

When we can answer this question honestly, we have found that to which we can be loyal. To all else we are respectful, compassionate, and merciful.

Ponder Poetry

I Am or I Have?

Chicago, 5.2015

Yesterday I spoke words.
"I am depressed."
For the first time.
Aloud.
For another to hear.
She already knew.
She has known
For seven years.
Two days ago,
I finally accepted
the reality that my life
would continue to be a mess
until I accepted fact.
But I resisted.
Not "I am depressed."
Instead, "I struggle with depression."
A simple phrase formulated
And accepted.
A burden lifted.
Not just "I have depression."
I manage depression.
I struggle with depression
like someone struggles with addiction.
I've taken way too long to admit,
to own this reality.
Seven years of therapy
Four years of medication—no more
How many years of signs?
Reviewing my life
From the lens of depression,
I clearly see threads running
through the fabric of my existence.

Exploration Studio 13: Cultivate

San Diego, California

Find Your Voice

MAKE.

Make a mistake: Failing is okay.

Make up your mind: Agonizing gets you nowhere.

Make up with someone: Life is too short to hold a grudge.

Make believe: Imagination brings awareness.

Make a difference: Affect the life of another.

Make a decision: Life is rarely that serious.

Make space: Allow for laughter and dance.

Make music: Sing a song from your soul.

Make love not war.

Be Well

MASSAGE.

While living in Hong Kong, I spent some time taking parents who were Vietnamese refugees detained in camps to visit their hospitalized children. One day, I held a toddler whose parent could not join us. The toddler in the next bed began to cry, and the child I held strained toward her. The child in my arms reached down and began to massage the other's ear. Within seconds, the crying stopped. No words were exchanged. The touch soothed her soul.

Body: If you've ever had a full-body massage, you know how relaxing and pampering it feels. But when you can't get in for a massage, try some at-home tricks. *Note: I am not a medical professional, but I've learned that drinking plenty of water after any massage is important to flush the toxins being released in your body.*

Foot and hand massage: Use your fingers or a simple wooden tool, buy inexpensive massaging slippers, or use an electronic option. You can find a reflexology map online if you want to know which points on the feet and hands correspond to which internal organs. I enjoy walking the rock path in my backyard. I've purposely included various sizes to hit different spots on my feet and like to run cool rain barrel water on the rocks during the summer months.

Stomach massage: A natural medicine doctor taught me to massage my torso in three sections to stimulate good digestion. For each section, place one hand on top of the other, gently press the top palm down on the other, and massage slowly in 30 clockwise circles.

Face and scalp massage (including the ears): A good scalp massage is my main reason for getting a haircut! Light, circular fingertip pressure on your face or scalp feels fabulous!

If you have a family member or friend (even a child) to help, try these:

Back pounding or walking: With the outside edge of your hand, chop back and forth and up and down the back. Or simply ask someone who isn't too heavy to walk slowly on your back.

Spoons: Dip the edge of a soup spoon in cool water and rub it along the back of the neck. The skin turns bright pink, but the tension release is immediate.

Mind: Massage can also be defined as: "to manipulate to get a more acceptable result." What old tapes or messages could use a little massaging? What new thoughts will encourage and energize you? Simply changing an "I should" to an "I could" allows you the power of choice.

Spirit: Experience tells me a good massage is great for emotional well-being. When I'm feeling glum and out of sorts, a hand, foot, or scalp massage often lifts my spirit. I might also massage my spirit by listening to meditative music, going for a walk, or calling a friend.

The way I look at it, massage is a healthy alternative to emotional eating, drinking too much, taking drugs, or wallowing in misery. Why not give it a try?

Choose Joy

Don't be afraid to trust and go where your joy takes you.

Anita Moorjani

This idea can be frightening. Just trust. It conjures up images of the old trust falls popular during high school retreats in the 1970s. One person stands behind the other and expects the person in front to fall backward into their arms: "Trust me."

But life isn't a trust fall that will result in a bruised tailbone if it fails. The stakes are much higher.

While we've all heard stories of those who made the incredible decision to walk away from a corporate job to follow their dreams and made millions, for every millionaire, how many more have experienced chaos and financial failure?

Don't get me wrong—I'm definitely all for walking away from toxic or dangerous situations. And I salute everyone wanting to be their own boss.

But going where your joy takes you doesn't mean you need to abandon all life structures and instantaneously jump all in to find your bliss while "the rest of you be damned."

Sometimes going where joy leads can mean taking small steps, making plans, taking precautionary measures, and moving slowly toward your goals and dreams.

You must trust yourself to know which method will work for you.

The important words, in my opinion, in Anita Moorjani's quote are, "Don't be afraid."

Making decisions rooted in fear often leads to pain and sorrow. Operating from fear keeps us from listening to our own or others' wisdom.

GO—quickly or slowly or in starts and stops—just be not afraid.

Move with Music
<u>Try</u>
Colbie Caillat

Challenge Your Perspective

Are you a person of faith?

信

person 人 word 言

My Chinese language teacher in Taiwan one day explained that her husband's parents had wholeheartedly embraced Christianity after the influence of a very persuasive missionary, but that her husband was not Christian because they needed one child to remain Buddhist so he could continue to honor the ancestors, burn paper money, and appease the gods—just in case Christianity wasn't the true religion.

Faith is believing what we cannot see or know for certain.

When someone speaks about faith, we immediately think of religion. But we have faith in so much more.

We have faith in many things: faith in ourselves. Faith in one another. Faith in God. Our lives depend on faith, even in mundane things like traffic laws, social norms, and modern medicine for curing disease.

Faith in the day that lies ahead wakes us up in the morning. Faith that tomorrow will be a better day is the lullaby singing us to sleep each night.

The Chinese word for *faith* is the radical for *person* 人 next to the character for *word* or *speech* 言.

We can have faith if a person's word is believable. Are they a person of their word? Is their word good?

Can others have faith in us? We must ask ourselves if our word is good. Can we be trusted? Do we do what we say we will?

Most importantly, do we have faith in ourselves?

Faith makes sense when the word we have heard, the word we have come to believe in—be it our own, that of a loved one, or that of God—matches our life experience.

Each broken promise, each "I love you" betrayed, makes faith in ourselves, another, or God more difficult. When word and experience collide, faith is weakened, trust is broken, and life becomes limiting.

Ponder Poetry

Transition

Chicago, 2014

i ate M&Ms for breakfast.
Yep. M&Ms. Peanut.

Leftovers from the night before
when i ate M&Ms
as a late-night snack. Crispy.

And that was left over from the earlier,
"Gotta pick up my kid at 10 pm
so i deserve a treat" snack.
A Butterfinger bar.

To be fair, i had a very nutritious lunch.
The logic i create
Around my self-destruction astounds me.

But i have been here before
In transition
Too many times.

My life is transition.
i am exhausted.

Exploration Studio 14: Surge

Marina, Martinez, California

Find Your Voice

NAME.

Our given name plays a part in defining who we are and how we relate to the world. As the seventh of eight children, I often heard my name at the end of a string my mother rattled through before landing on mine. I was given nicknames: Tiger, Arnie Pig, Big Clumsy Elephant. When I became a sister, I chose a new name. Later, I was given a Chinese name. When I married, I took on my husband's last name.

Beyond names, we also have labels. In many circles, I'm known as my husband's wife or my child's mother. We all have labels that become part of our identity: wife, mother, teacher, cook, entrepreneur. How we introduce ourselves and what others call us matters because it dictates how we relate to the world. How do we allow others to name us?

Remember that *name* is also a verb. We have the power to name that which impacts us.

If we NAME our emotions, we can identify them as separate from ourselves. They have their own names. We aren't one and the same. I am not "angry." I am Janet, and I feel anger. When we can name—rather than judge—our emotions, we take on an entirely new power over them.

If we NAME the labels others give us, we decide what is true and how much power they hold. Am I "scattered" or "multitalented"? Am I "bossy" or "a leader"?

If we NAME the injustices in this world, we can begin to make change because we can speak about the action and consequence. We name the "-ism" for what it is and work to eradicate that "-ism," not attack the people perpetuating it.

When we name something, we can decide if it is holding us back or propelling us forward. We can choose how we relate to it and whether it defines us. When we name something, we have the power.

Be Well

NOTICE.

Sometimes to take care of ourselves, all we need to do is notice.

Body:

Notice the aches and pains. Notice the beautiful and not so beautiful. Notice the signs of aging. If these physical realities you notice evoke thoughts and emotion, notice those, too.

Mind:

Notice your thoughts. Where do they turn when you are alone or in a crowd? When you are busy or bored? When you are exercising or relaxing?

Spirit:

Notice your feelings. Notice what impacts your moods. What triggers sadness, happiness, anger, fear, guilt, anxiety, excitement, courage? What brings you joy and fills you with gratitude?

Notice but don't judge.

Take note and ASK, BRUSH, CELEBRATE, DANCE, EXHALE, FAST, GINGER, HUG, IMAGINE, JINK, KINDLE, LAUGH, MASSAGE.

Take note and choose how you will respond.

Remember that a musical note that stands alone is simply a noise, but, when strategically strung together, notes make beautiful music.

Choose Joy

Learning to live in the present moment is part of the path of joy.

Sarah Ban Breathnach

I'm reminded of a moment I had with my teenage daughter as she shared how Leo Tolstoy's *War and Peace* talks about calculus and the fact that in any given instance nothing moves (a point on a graph), but over time (many points on a graph), we see motion.

If at any given moment all is still, how do we learn to live in that stillness?

The present moment is fleeting. A moment in time is just that—a moment of stillness. Living in a moment of stillness is great if we are meditating, but what about other hours of the day?

I like to consider "the present moment" as more than a literal moment.

We have 86,400 seconds in a day. Do we have 86,400 moments? Or is a 24-hour day the present moment? Or is a moment an event like a scene in a movie or book, like the "moment" I had with my daughter?

We are never guaranteed another moment whether that is 5 seconds, 86,400 seconds, or any number of seconds in between.

We have only now. Whether we are meditating, eating, chatting with a loved one, making love, yelling at the driver in front of us, or crying our eyes out, we have only this moment in time.

Given this, do we want to spend *this* moment holding grudges, regretting, or fretting over the past or worrying, having anxiety, or fretting about the future?

To live in the present moment is to GO ALL IN. And if we go all in, regardless of what that moment is, we open ourselves to experience JOY.

To experience true JOY doesn't mean to be ecstatic all the time but to be fully immersed in a moment, embracing and honoring what is.

Move with Music
Run the World
Beyoncé

Challenge Your Perspective

Are you narrow-minded?

气量小的

air 气 capacity 量 small 小 someone who 的

To be narrow-minded is to have small capacity for air.

The English word *narrow-minded* is itself quite graphic. We can easily envision a person whose mind has closed off to new ideas or ways different from one's own.

For me, the Chinese phrase for *narrow-minded* implies a bit more. I think of it as having an asthmatic attitude toward life.

When our minds are narrow, we are closed off to new ideas, but we can still function. But if we have a small capacity for air, we cannot breathe. And when we cannot breathe, we endanger our lives, our very being.

Even thinking about moments when I've been narrow-minded makes my muscles tighten, my shoulders hunch, and my jaw set.

But if we take full, deep breaths, letting in more air, everything relaxes. When air flows freely and our bodies soften, it is tough to remain narrow-minded.

Ponder Poetry

Every Perfect Moment

12.31.2016

Every day. Every hour. Every moment.
Is the beginning of a new year
filled with power, possibility, potential, promise.
Is not this moment, this hour, this day *new?*
We are not who we just were—
for every moment, hour, day
has power, possibility, potential, promise.
To change who we are.
We are made new
With every action and reaction
With every thought and desire
With every day, hour, moment.
Why wait until—until what?
Until the moment gets away? Until when?
Every thing. Every person. Every moment is—
Is what?
Perfect?
Is not this moment, this hour, this day *perfect?*
Is not every day? Every hour. Every moment. Perfect?
For something?
For this is the only day, hour, moment we are given.

Exploration Studio 15: Shine

Sunset from an airplane

Find Your Voice

OBEY.

At first glance, the idea of asking someone to obey might feel counterintuitive to the idea of finding your voice. After all, doesn't obedience imply doing what someone else asks or even demands? To obey, don't we need to ignore or repress our own ideas and desires?

The word *obey* comes from the Latin *oboedire*, which is "ob" meaning "in the direction of" and "audiere" meaning "to hear."

The call "to obey" can be a call to "pay attention," to "listen"—not only to others, the "should" of society, and arbitrary, often oppressive concepts—but to our gut, our deepest desires, our divine power.

I am not suggesting that we allow for anarchy and chaos and never follow the basic rules of society, but I am suggesting that perhaps we take the time and space to listen within.

Are we living a life that makes sense to us, that sits right with our conscience and our own potential? Or are we allowing old tapes, fear, or negative environments and relationships to overpower our own voice?

May I suggest that if you are unhappy in your relationships, your work, or the direction your life has taken that you take a moment to obey, to listen—not to all the outside voices but to your own.

Be Well

OPT-in or OPT-out.

Once I was registered for a networking event with other consultants. I don't attend too many of these types of events, but this one was just blocks from my home, rather than in downtown Chicago. I was interested in the topic and had the time. It all made sense.

Until 20 minutes before start time when I was walking to my room to change and head out.

In a snap, I decided not to go. I returned to the couch, told my husband I had changed my mind, and relaxed for the evening. I opted in and then I opted out.

Body: Our bodies will often tell us when it is time to opt-in or opt-out. Do we listen?

Mind: Do you pressure yourself with *shoulds*? Do you do things out of an unwarranted sense of obligation or guilt?

Spirit: When something we do doesn't feed our souls, it is time to let it go. What do you need to bless and release?

Self-care and wellness are about choice. While some things are obligatory, like the April 15th tax deadline in the United States, many activities, hobbies, habits, and events optional. We can opt-in or opt-out for our own good.

Choose Joy

EN-joy your day.

Janet Cobb

A few years ago, as my career imploded and I faced my fifth life reinvention, the polite phrase, "Have a nice day," struck me.

I suddenly realized that each day, in all its promised messiness, was going to be what it was. I could sit passively and hope to "have" a nice one, begrudging anything not nice about it.

Or I could be proactive—and EN-joy my day. That "EN" is the energy I choose to put into it.

I have the power to infuse any day or moment with JOY. I do not need to wait passively or simply react to whatever happens. I can decide to enjoy the day, regardless of what happens.

Move with Music
Beautiful

Carole King

Challenge Your Perspective

Are you obedient?

聽話

listen 聽 speech 話

Obedience often implies a relationship of service or servitude. You must do what another person says. Children must be obedient to their parents, students to their teachers—a clear difference in power dynamics.

I like to consider the parts of the Chinese word for *listen* when I think of *obedience*. When I was learning to write the word, I noticed immediately the *ear* 耳 and *heart* 心. Listening involves our ears and our heart. The character also includes the symbols for *king* (the one who historically demands obedience), *ten*, and *eye* (which indicates the need to be very observant as if we were watching with ten eyes).

So, the question becomes, if we are truly paying attention, watching with ten eyes, and listening with our ears and our hearts—what are we being called to do?

In the convent, I took three vows: chastity, poverty, and obedience. During our training, we studied these vows to better understand the life to which we were committing. We had one or two lessons on chastity and poverty. The basic messages were "sex is bad" and "money is good if we share it." I had more than TEN lessons on obedience.

Years later, when learning Chinese, I had my "Aha!" moment. I realized the woman who had designed these lessons was a control freak. My entire world turned upside down. I suddenly noticed how she manipulated the young women just beginning their training. I understood the previous ten years of my life very differently.

My process of leaving the convent was more complex than learning the Chinese word for *obey*, but I found clarity in realizing that I had reduced my obedience to the whims of one person.

When we are embroiled in emotionally abusive relationships, it can be difficult to see, hear, and trust our eyes, ears, and heart. We question ourselves instead of the world around us.

But to be truly obedient, we must see with ten eyes and hear with our hearts—all that is being presented to us. We must be obedient, first and foremost to our own hearts.

Ponder Poetry

A Defining Moment

April 1994
thirteen years
no more a nun.
Starting life over at 30.
Chicago, secondhand clothes,
prayer books in hand.
no job, no credit history, no real resume.
A cousin's couch to sleep on.
A defining moment.

June 2000
Marriage, two children
Need support.
Quit our jobs, head to California
Find a house, employment
near family.
A defining moment.

October 2004
My daughter wakes me.
Vomit covers her bed, her wall,
the junk dropped around
a bedroom floor.
A defining moment.

May 2007
Philosophical differences.
We quit our jobs, list house,
Returned to Chicago
three children in tow
real estate market tanks.
search for work, a place to live.
A defining moment.

May 2009
A man lying on the sidewalk
unconscious
Me running late.
Call 911 and wait.
My son, content to inform his teacher
the reason for his tardiness.
A defining moment.

December 2011
Drive children from school.
A teen girl head-locked into the icy ground.
Stop the car. Pull over.
Approach the teen boys.
A defining moment.

January 2012
See it coming.
Prepare collaterally.
Lose my job.
Reality stings.
A defining moment.

What are your defining moments?

Exploration Studio 16: Rejuvenate

Phoenix, Arizona

Find Your Voice

PROTECT. PAUSE. PACE. PERSEVERE.

In the moment we realize that we need to find our voice, we can sometimes allow our need to be heard to overpower us and our relationships. With each defining moment, each time we have the courage to announce our needs, say "no" or "yes," our courage grows.

Speaking up becomes almost addictive.

The temptation can be to point fingers, attack those we perceive as stifling us, and accuse others of silencing us. Don't get me wrong. If we have suffered abuse, we must remove ourselves by any means possible. We must first PROTECT ourselves.

Once we are certain of our physical and emotional safety, we can take a moment to PAUSE, take a moment to consider the part we played in giving over our voice and allowing ourselves to be silenced.

We can then begin to articulate the best next steps and to PACE ourselves for change. The ones we love and who love us can support us in our desire to find our voice and our peace. Pacing ourselves can open the door to discovering new possibilities to try and to fail and to try again.

The change will feel like a roller coaster ride of ups and downs, but if we PERSEVERE, we will find our voice, our peace, and our joy.

Be Well

PAMPER.

To pamper, according to a simple internet search, is "to indulge with every attention, comfort, and kindness; spoil."

When you check *Merriam-Webster*, the archaic definition is "to cram with rich food: GLUT."

If to pamper means "to indulge with every attention," how do you pamper yourself without becoming gluttonous?

Body:

- A bubble bath and candles?
- A full-body massage?
- A bowl full of delicious salad with just the right amount of dressing?
- A run or a swim?
- A big piece of chocolate cake with ice cream?

Mind:

- A comedy show?
- A horror film?
- A good book with a cup of tea?
- A solid discussion with a close friend?

Spirit:

- A day at the beach?
- A glass of wine?
- A moment of meditation?
- A chat with a trusted confidant?

Find that *thing* that makes you feel special, cozy, relaxed, energized, or alive. Enjoy your indulgence in gratitude.

Choose Joy

There's a whole lot of joy just waiting for you to find it.

Unknown

If joy is waiting to be found, what can we do to find it?

Some ideas:

- Take deep breaths.
- Meditate.
- Go for a walk, run or bike ride.
- Spend time in nature.
- Find room for play, creativity, relaxation.
- Honor your emotions.

Are you open to the joy in your life waiting to be found?

If not, why not?

If yes, do you have a habit or "trick" to tap into JOY?

Move with Music

This One's for the Girls
Martina McBride

Challenge Your Perspective

Do you have patience?

忍

edge of the blade 刃 heart 心

I used to tell students that any research project entails searching again and again—a concept unknown to the "Google it" generation. They can find anything with the press of a button.

I tried to impress upon them, as was impressed upon me, that success takes preparation, hard work, and time. But we live in a world of social media influencers who make millions simply by photographing every minute of their day. Entire generations have been raised on *American Idol* and other reality shows that can catapult someone from obscurity to fame in mere weeks.

For most of us, reaching our goals and designing the life we desire takes patience.

The Chinese word for *patience* is a knife blade over the heart. The Latin root of the English word comes from "suffering."

Patience can be painful. Sometimes excruciating.

But patience doesn't have to be passive. And patience doesn't have to be quiet.

To be patient is to acknowledge that the result, the reality, and the vision we desire will take time. Patience gives us hope to keep going.

But during that time, we don't have to sit idly by.

We can continue to work toward our desired goal. We can take steps to move the needle. We can gather others who believe in our cause and support our dreams.

And, with a knife blade to our heart, we grow stronger.

Ponder Poetry

Motherhood

Chicago, 4.8.12

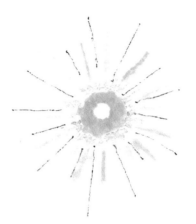

We Wait.
To have children. 9 months. Years.
1 trimester. 2 trimesters.3 trimesters.
For the beauty, the joy,
The fear to be complete.
We Wait.
In Fear.
Fear that we will never be good enough.
Fear that we will screw up the life of this precious little one.
Or that someone else will.
God forbid someone else does.
We Wait.
To hold them close, forever. Never let them go.
We Wait.
Yet they begin.
To walk, to talk, to say NO
And yes & maybe & darn & crap because
Maybe we just don't agree.
We Wait.
We stand proud, sit quietly
Searching our souls for why
Praying for safety and happiness.
Struggling to let them go and hold them close
And teach them a lesson
And convince them we love them no matter what.
We Wait.
They call for advice
And the days turn brighter
We Wait.
To come by for a visit. Say thank you. I'm sorry.
And we wait.
Until that moment
Until we realize that we are that same child
To the mom we ignored at 13,
Argued with at 18, knew better than at 23,
Shared our dreams with at 30.
Just maybe we realize in time
Before she is gone forever
We Wait.
And we tell her how much we love her. Or we don't.
Instead. We Wait. And pray she knows.

Exploration Studio 17: Marvel

Lake Tahoe 2018

Find Your Voice

QUESTION.

When we are in search of our own voice, we might strike out against things that we previously accepted. We might feel like nothing makes sense, even like life itself is falling apart.

When seeking our own voice, we might need to pause, but I suggest that during the pause we begin to question.

Question everything you remember, everything you've been taught, everything you believe.

Question so that you can answer—again. So that you can answer with your own voice. So that you can own your answers.

Some of your answers might change. Some of your answers might surprise you. Some of your answers might scare the crap out of you. But they will be your answers.

And your answers might make others feel threatened, or frightened, or angry.

But remember, your choices need not invalidate theirs. And their choices do not invalidate yours. Each person must find answers for themselves.

Question everything.

Be Well

QUIET.

> Your body.
> Your mind.
> Your spirit.

Choose Joy

Look within. Be still. Free from fear and attachment, know the sweet joy of living in the way.

Buddha

I began gathering quotes about joy years ago. As I scrolled through the list to decide which ones to share here, I was struck by the wide variety of folks on the list: Buddha, Mother Teresa, Sri Sri, Deepak Chopra, Theodore Roosevelt, Brené Brown, Rumi, Joseph Campbell. The list goes on.

The basic ideas in the quotes remain the same:

- Be still.
- Look within.
- Choose joy.
- Practice gratitude.
- Let go of fear.

This leads me to wonder.

If so many folks from different spiritual, political, social, and personal backgrounds are offering similar thoughts, can they all be wrong?

If they are all pointing in the same direction, how can we not believe them and practice what they preach?

Move with Music
Scars to Your Beautiful

Alessia Cara

Challenge Your Perspective

Are you prudent?

慎

heart 忄 true 真

I was told more than once in my teen and young adult life that I needed to be more prudent—to know the right thing to say or do at the right time.

Loving my own spontaneity, I often acted impulsively (and sometimes still do).

My words and actions weren't mean or hurtful. Even so, I was often admonished after doing something I thought another would value—sharing a token of appreciation, offering a suggestion, or expressing exuberance at someone else's idea.

When I was admonished, I was tempted to shrink, to cower, to never trust my impulses.

Through the years, I've learned how to take a moment, to pause and think before I speak or act, to consider how my words and actions might impact others.

But I've also committed to acting prudently. For this, I must balance being genuine and "true to my heart" while being aware that others might see things very differently.

Their truth may not be the same as mine.

When we recognize that every person's experience is unique and that a word or action that we might appreciate or enjoy could be disruptive or hurtful to someone else, we will step more gingerly and speak more tenderly.

And when we screw up, we listen, apologize, and carry with us a lesson for the next time.

Ponder Poetry

Hammers & Harps

Santa Cruz, CA, 2.25.1982

The Darkness sets all around.
The night is still.
My heart beats to a slow pounding hammer.
All is finished.
My soul, lying limp, lifeless
No light shines in all the Earth
Despair, deep despair.
Yet hear!
There is a sound stirring within
A small pitter patter as if rain falls.
Still darkness. Then silence.
A light, a small flickering.
The darkness cannot hold light.
White! Bright!
The brightness fades
The glitter lingers on
echoing noise, flickering beams
fragrance fills the night.
Sweetness, sweet as honey yet so bitter.
Trumpets blast!
The stone falls. There is a light
Sweetness within
My soul awakens
The hammer is gone. Scars left behind.
Divine life within me. A newness.
I am empty, yet FULL.
I have nothing but ALL.
Glory. Salvation.
My heart beats to the music.
Harps play.
My freedom is won.

Exploration Studio 18: Roar

Backyard Fire, Chicago, Illinois

Find Your Voice

ROAR!

In my childhood, Helen Reddy's song "I Am Woman" was very popular. "I am woman, hear me roar..." When my daughter was in high school, Katy Perry's song "Roar" reminded me of Reddy's.

One traditional form of meditation in the Catholic church is the practice of *Lectio Divina*, divine reading.

Whether you enjoy the music genre of these two songs or not, perhaps reflecting on the lyrics will help you find your reason to roar—to declare to the world that you are loud and proud and ready to conquer the world.

For copyright reasons, I cannot post the lyrics here, but you can find them online.

I Am Woman by Helen Reddy

ROAR by Katy Perry

If these two songs don't speak to you, ponder the words to songs, poems, or scripture that do.

Be Well

RIGHT-SIZE.

Stress and tension can come from the mismatch between what we think should happen and what we're actually capable of, based on our limited time, resources and the certain gifts and talents we possess.

When we right-size, we create harmony between life's various elements. We see how each aspect is interdependent on the other.

Body:

Do the beauty, fashion, weight-loss industries have us believing that our body isn't good enough? Do we expect more from our body than is fair or realistic?

Mind:

The stimuli from social media and 24-hour news, the bombardment of information, the proliferation of pressure to always achieve MORE, and the fear of missing out can wreak havoc. Do we overtax our minds?

Spirit:

Could the "need to get straight As" and the "everyone gets a trophy" mentality have led to a tug-of-war in our souls? Do we desire perfection or fear failure?

When we begin to right-size our expectations for ourselves and others, we open the door to gratitude and appreciation for all we have. With gratitude and appreciation comes new perspective.

Perhaps we don't have to be perfect. Perhaps we don't have to *have it all*. Perhaps less is more and perhaps we ARE good enough.

And, in that middle way, we find bliss.

Choose Joy

People who exude joy encourage the joy in me.

Maya Angelou

Much like the Moon reflects the light of the Sun, the joy of another can bring out the joy in us.

Even through clouds.

Think of someone or something that makes you smile.

Surround yourself with joyful people.

Today, if you struggle to exude joy may you bask in the reflection of another's.

Move with Music
Beautiful
Christina Aguilera

Challenge Your Perspective

Where do you find rest?

放心

put down 放 heart 心

The Chinese word for *relax*, as in to not be concerned and to let go of worry, is *put down* 放 and *heart* 心. The expression was very common when I lived in Taiwan and Hong Kong. I heard it often.

Every time I was struck by the imagery of putting down your heart. Imagine simply leaving a heavy heart to rest somewhere safe and secure.

Many people find rest for their hearts in their religious faith.

I am reminded of the words of Jesus: "Don't let your hearts be troubled" (John 14:1) and "Come to me, all you who are weary and burdened, and I will give you rest" (Matthew 11:28).

Others find comfort in rituals.

Rituals can often be beautiful exercises in putting down your heart.

I'm reminded of the practice, for some in the Jewish tradition, of placing folded pieces of paper representing prayers in the crevices of the Western Wall.

I think of the placing of fruit on the ancestral altars in many Buddhist homes and the placing of flowers on gravesites across the United States.

Ritual offers us a place to put down our hearts.

If you don't find your rest in religion, where and how do you put down your cares and worries? Are you a non-worrier by nature? Do you meditate, practice Yoga, smoke weed, exercise, journal, chat with a trusted friend? Do you binge-watch your favorite show for a temporary reprieve?

Do you have a tradition, ritual, practice, or habit that gives your heart rest?

Ponder Poetry

Roar of a Wave

Hong Kong, 1990

Combing the beach to find
A precious gem, a special one,
Gently lift and gaze in awe—
The roar of a wave echoes in my ear.
That sacred moment of sharing—
The seashell and ocean from which it came,
Comes only through the death of one
Willing to be emptied and tossed ashore.
The security and peace once known
To the creature in the depths
Is abandoned to grant serenity,
Moments of inspiration for me.
As I caress the shell, I ponder.
Think of the ocean; hear its voice.
A gentle plea:
May I be a remembrance of grace.
When others plod the sands of life
Seeking that precious gem, the special one,
If, by chance, they stumble upon me,
Let them feel welcome, find their voice,
And turn their gaze inward in awe—
The roar of a wave echoing in their ear.

Exploration Studio 19: Fulfill

Sedona, Arizona

Find Your Voice

SCREAM.

Have you ever pondered the difference between *scream* and *shout?*

I don't think they are the same thing. For me, shouting feels more positive. I shout at exciting sporting events, or when I'm trying to get someone's attention and they aren't close by. I shout my truth from the mountain top.

But I scream when I can't find my voice, when I can't pinpoint the cause of my pain, when I am afraid to listen to my heart, often for fear of the consequences if I do speak up. For many years in the convent, I didn't have the courage to speak up and honor my truth. Expressing emotion or confusion was frowned upon.

I discovered that one of the best places to scream was in the car, driving at full speed on the expressway. I turned up the radio and screamed at the top of my lungs. Sometimes high pitched, other times with deep guttural moans. Looking back, I realize how much unacknowledged pain I carried.

My screams came from deep within the soul.

While I still get upset and angry, and I cry and even yell from time to time, I've dug deep to find my voice and speak my truth. And, although I use the expression, "I wanted to scream," I realize that I no longer have the need.

Be Well

STRETCH.

Body:

As our bodies age, stretching becomes a critical part of staying healthy and living well. If you begin to feel stiff or something begins to ache, try giving it a good stretch. Stretching releases toxins and allows us to move more freely.

When we stretch our bodies through exercise, we experience heightened blood flow and shots of adrenaline and dopamine which energize us.

Mind:

Stretching the mind is critical to the preservation of compassion and empathy in our world today. Throughout my life, I've lived between two worlds: white child growing up in a black neighborhood, poor child attending a wealthy school, young nun living with elderly nuns, an American living in Asia.

Although we were all raised Catholic, at one point within my own family, I was a Catholic nun, one brother was a Baptist minister, one sister attended a Community Bible Church, another brother married a Mormon, and several siblings practiced no religion at all.

I've always considered myself to be open to new ideas and capable of listening to others' opinions. But the more I can stretch my mind to know and understand that which is different and unfamiliar, the better person I will be.

Spirit:

To stretch our spirit is to have compassion.

The word used for compassion in the parables of the Prodigal Son and the Good Samaritan was *splagchnoisomai*, which means "to let one's innards embrace the feeling or situation of another."

This may not always feel good because to have compassion sometimes means we must "suffer with" another. But I believe with every fiber of my being that unless and until we each learn *splagchnoisomai*, atrocities from hate and intolerance will abound.

Choose Joy

You cannot struggle your way to joy.
Struggle and joy are not on the same channel. You JOY your way to JOY.
Abraham Hicks

Many years ago, during my first "midlife crisis" (at age 30), I was struggling hard emotionally, spiritually, and physically. I had the good fortune to experience a 30-day retreat in the tradition of the Spiritual Exercises of St. Ignatius.

Early in the retreat, I was directed to reflect on the story of 12-year-old Jesus remaining behind in the temple when he and his parents had traveled to Jerusalem.

These Spiritual Exercises rely heavily on the imagination, so participants place themselves inside the biblical scenes, taking on the perspective of one character or another. So, I asked Joseph the same question Jesus had.

"Why were you searching for me?" he asked (Luke 2:49).

In my imagination, I listened for Joseph's response.

Joseph explained that the timing wasn't right, and Jesus asked, "How will I know when the time is right?"

And Joseph lovingly replied, "When you are no longer agitated."

Not being agitated doesn't mean that everything will be easy or pleasant or hunky-dory. Not being agitated means that we embrace the power of choice and remain present to the moment. Without agitation, we can act quickly but not in a hurry. We can trust ourselves to make good decisions.

If we accept the present situation—regardless of how messed up it might be—not in apathy or tolerance of evil and immorality, but with the joy of knowing BETTER is POSSIBLE, we can see our way to that new possibility. We can joy our way to joy.

Move with Music
Confident
Demi Lovato

Challenge Your Perspective

Is sex life-giving?

性

heart 忄 life, life-giving 生

Sex has been a taboo subject for most of my life.

Like many my age, our families didn't discuss it except to tell us it was something married people did. Beyond that, I had a vague impression it was something to be tolerated.

The convent shunned it. Of course, sex was holy if you were married, but a vow of chastity was the "better choice" because it made me the Bride of Christ.

The Chinese word for *sex* combines the *heart* 忄 with the symbol for *life* or *life-giving* 生. Learning this word gave me a new perspective on sex.

At the time, I was a twenty-something young woman vowed to a life of chastity with no plan to ever engage in sex.

I pondered the juxtaposition of the heart next to the idea of life and giving life. I wondered.

Does having sex give birth to the heart? Do our hearts drive us to desire sex? Is sex meaningless without our hearts being involved? Or is sex the act by which our hearts give birth to another human being?

I don't remember ever answering these questions. Perhaps they are rhetorical. Perhaps they, in part, led to my eventually leaving the convent.

But given both the taboo nature of sex and the various iterations of sexual revolution through the decades, I think it is still worth pondering for ourselves:

Is sex life-giving for me?

If yes, hallelujah!

If not, why not? If not, what can I do to change that for myself?

Ponder Poetry

Snap.

Chicago, 2.16.2015

He just snapped!
Just snap out of it.
Aw, Snap!
The instant
The moment
The point in time
Drastic change
The tipping point.
Snap.
The a-ha
The light bulb.
The snap
Of perfect sense
Or falling to pieces
Or striking a chord
Of clarity
Or disaster.
Snap.
Doesn't happen
For those struggling
With depression.
Nothing snaps.
Instead, a constant
Clawing grasping, pining struggle
To stay connected
To people
Places. Passions
Around them.
Like tug-of-war
A love hate
relationship with their **Me.**

.

Not you.
It isn't about You.
Or the work
Or the stress.
Or the job.
The war is within.
Controlled by the uncontrollable.
Uncontrolled by the controllable.
Managed.
Camouflaged.
Hidden by the struggle.
Every ounce of energy,
Of courage
Of pain
Becomes the next step
But what looks like
Snap
Is the volcano
Infection
Emotional tumor
Growing
Screaming
Struggling
To be free.
Snap.
Don't wait.
Accept the struggle.
Celebrate the struggle.
Be at peace with your *Me.*

Exploration Studio 20: Integrate

Coronado Beach, San Diego, California

Find Your Voice

TREAT.

"Treat others as they want to be treated" (*The Platinum Rule*, Michael O'Connor and Tony Alessandra). More than the Golden Rule, which teaches us to treat others as we want to be treated, the Platinum Rule takes compassion to the next level.

But what does treating others with compassion and respect have to do with finding your voice?

Often when we are struggling to be true to ourselves and find our voice, we become a little self-centered. In an effort to protect our sanity and assert our independence, we can become egocentric. And rightly so. We need to treat ourselves well if we are going to move forward.

Treat yourself to a lazy day, a good book, a strong drink, a luncheon with your gal pals, a vacation, a walk—whatever helps you transition to the other side. My old favorite for tough times as a teenager: vanilla ice cream, Nacho Cheese Doritos and Orange Fanta.

The treats ebb and flow from less healthy to extremely healthy options. And through it all, we come to learn how we want to be treated. We begin to articulate how we will allow others to treat us, and we recognize that we must treat others as they want to be treated.

When we learn how to treat ourselves and to teach others how we want to be treated, we will better see, hear, and understand how others want to be treated.

Bronze: If they are not bothering you, don't bother them. Mind your business.
Silver: Do not do unto others as you would not have them do unto you.
Golden: Do unto others as you would have them do unto you.
Platinum: Treat others as they want to be treated.

Be Well

TARGET.

To target is to "select as an object of attention or attack."

What are you aiming for? What is your bull's-eye? Why do you do what you do? Without a target, it is difficult to aim.

Without a target, we are likely to wander or flail.

Body:

Setting targets for our body is simple. (Accomplishing them, maybe not so much.) Target heart rate, target cholesterol and sugar numbers, target weight. Target routines, sleep or eating patterns, a distance you want to run or a Yoga pose to master.

But in setting these targets, let's keep them right-sized, and let's love ourselves along the way.

Mind:

When we set out to expand our mind in some way by learning a new skill or taking up a new hobby, knowing why we are doing it can give us a sense of direction. Is this to generate revenue, to keep my mind sharp in old age, to better understand the world in which I live?

Once we know our target, we can set our plan for "attack" and get it done.

Spirit:

To be sure, having a target isn't always about getting something done.

I think of choosing "to be" rather than "to do" as having a target of attention.

Sometimes life needs to be about getting NOTHING DONE and just being.

But if we don't set that target, we're likely to busy ourselves with meaningless tasks because we don't know HOW to relax.

For the "list-happy, get-things-done" types among us, perhaps making a target list of "attention" rather than "attack" is just what we need to be well.

Choose Joy

Remember that your natural state is joy.

Wayne Dyer

If our natural state is joy, what robs us of it?

What misdirects us? What keeps us from experiencing the joy that is ours?

I'm confident that sitting here, writing this reflection, I could list any number of culprits: painful experiences, betrayal, worry about the future, fear of the unknown, childhood trauma, regrets of the past.

But, if we stop to think about it, only *CHOICE* keeps us from joy. Joy is my choice. Joy is your choice. We have the power to choose to experience joy.

Move with Music

Fight Song
Rachel Platten

Challenge Your Perspective

Do you decide or discern?

思

brain 囟 heart 心

In the United States, and perhaps in Western thought, the brain and the heart are distinct entities with distinct roles to play in our lives.

We have expressions like "use your head," when encouraging someone to think logically, and "follow your heart," when talking about feelings and emotions.

To think is to reason. We evaluate cause/effect, action/consequence. We think things through in order to decide.

In contrast, the Chinese word for *thought* combines the *brain* 囟 and the *heart* 心. The brain is placed over the heart, but together, using both, we ponder, consider, reflect, and think.

Often the dichotomy of head versus heart keeps us from making good decisions. We weigh pros and cons. We pit one against the other. Many popular personality tests reinforce this distinction. We think *or* we feel, as if we can't do both.

We act as if the head and the heart are in a competition to control our decisions and direct our lives. But what if our thinking was set upon the foundation of our heart? What if we allowed our hearts to guide our brains?

A more holistic approach would be to invite our brains and our hearts together to guide our thoughts. What if, instead of reasoning through a situation to make a decision, we wove our way through reason and emotion to discern.

By giving attention to both the logical, often linear, processes in our brains and the emotional, often less delineated, processes of our hearts, we will find that which gives peace and leads to joy even if it doesn't always "make sense" logically.

Ponder Poetry

Feminine Cycles

Chicago, 4.29.1994
Originally titled "On Beginning the 50th year"

Unknown and dark, still warm and secure
Creative energy slowly,
ever so gently shapes,
energizes, and enables love,
the catalyst,
not controlling
joyfully explodes new life.
A sign of home and promise.
Recreation remembers that womb
the love which enabled
and delicately energized
and her divine catalyst
slowly, gently,
ever so gently
offers the gift of co-creation
Brightness engulfs the child
Light but sometimes cold
safe yet often scared.
The bundle of life cradled in mother's arms
grows to forget the catalyst,
the gentle hand and warming touch.
Energy is blocked, fear embraced.
Struggles rage within to resist the unknown
Until quiet footsteps catch her unaware
Like a mantle wrapping her in peace
Of unknown dark tomorrows
We rejoice, amidst tears
for the heartbroken
the pain embraced; the life shared
to bring forth
new birth in our world.

Exploration Studio 21: Triumph

San Diego, California

Find Your Voice

UN-

Unbox.
What labels have you allowed to box you in? What boxes have you used to compartmentalize your life and keep you from feeling whole? What do you keep yourself from doing because it doesn't fit your outward persona?

Unbind.
What binds you up? What keeps you from growing? What stifles your voice? What fears or worries keep you wound up too tightly?

Unbar.
What keeps you feeling imprisoned and behind bars? What actions from the past are you still punishing yourself for? What freedoms do you deny yourself because of guilt?

Unwind.
Do you know how to relax and let go? Have you done anything a little "wild and crazy" lately? Or at least spontaneous? Are you afraid that if you let go you will lose control?

Unhinge.
Have you ever been unhinged? Is being unhinged always a negative? Have you ever bounced back when you came unhinged?

Be Well

ULULATE.

To ululate is to "howl or wail as an expression of strong emotion, typically grief."

When I came across this word, I was immediately transported to my days living in Taiwan.

More than once, from my window or my roof, I overlooked the wailing of men and women dressed in white (which being from the U.S. was reminiscent of the horrific KKK), standing at the front of a funeral procession. According to the locals I spoke with, a custom was to pay professional wailers to attend the funeral to express the grief of the family and friends left behind.

That experience, and the many funeral services I've attended for family and friends, convinced me that sometimes the only way to express our pain is to howl or wail.

But I also believe with all my soul that outside of the grief of death, many of us carry sharp grief—from the loss of a dream, a relationship, a sense of who we thought we were. But rather than ululate, we suffocate our feelings, trying to be strong and move on.

Body:

If we do not howl or wail when we need to, it will "eat away at us" and manifest in physical disease, leading to inexplicable aches and pains or more serious ailments.

Mind:

If we do not howl or wail when we need to, we may find ourselves constantly distracted and unable to concentrate, spewing frustration and anger in the wrong direction, or we might find ourselves spiraling into depression.

Spirit:

If we do not howl or wail when we need to, our souls will suffer. Grief is a heavy burden to carry, and when it is unacknowledged, it is even more likely to drag us down.

Let yourself grieve the losses you've experienced—be they physical, mental, or spiritual—no matter how minor others (or you) think they may be.

Please ULULATE before it is too late!

Choose Joy

We cannot cure the world of sorrows, but we can choose to live in joy.

Joseph Campbell

Some days, hearing about yet another act of violence or hatred, I wonder if focusing on joy is putting a bandage on a gaping wound. Is choosing joy a feeble attempt to ignore pain and sorrow—to live in delusion?

But joy is not found *within* the source of the sorrow.

Joy provides the strength within me to face the pain and do all I can to heal the wounded. Joy provides the courage to confront the causes of violence and hatred and to become part of the solution rather than part of the problem.

Joy provides the wisdom needed to speak or act to bring about change, big or small, when the opportunity arises. Joy provides hope for a better tomorrow. Joy provides light in the darkness of night.

Move with Music

Invincible

Kelly Clarkson

Challenge Your Perspective

Do you hate?

怨恨

to turn over when asleep 夗 heart 心 stubborn 恨

I have never quite understood the concept of hate.

Sure, I've said things like, "I hate it when…" or "Oh, I hate that!" about a given situation. But beyond the frenzied tantrums of my childhood when I may have shouted "I hate you!" at a playmate who upset me, I don't understand hate.

My mother drilled into me that if we hated something it meant that we wished for it the fires of eternal damnation.

Wow.

I could never wish that on anyone or anything. Right?

But when I think about hate from the perspective of the Chinese characters for hate, it gives me pause.

The characters for *hate* are derived from the word for "turn over when asleep" 夗 placed over the word for *heart* 心 and a heart is part of the word for *stubborn* (which is pictorially a person with a large eye looking back) 艮.

Without the fear of eternal damnation, this idea of hatred makes me think.

Do I ever lose sleep or toss and turn over my distaste for or dislike of someone or something they did? Do I dig my heels in, refusing to forgive someone? Am I stubborn in my opinions about anything or anyone?

When I think about hate from this angle, I'm not so confident that I have never "hated" anyone. Fortunately, not in recent memory.

But if we think about hate as being our stubborn selves tossing and turning in our sleep, we can notice that it does NOTHING to the object of our hate. Just as when we are angry with someone, the world keeps turning and their lives keep moving. With hatred, we spin.

By our insistence on looking back, reliving the moment that angered or hurt us, we get stuck.

Ponder Poetry

Don't Talk to Strangers

Strangers.
Don't talk to strangers.
We teach our children.
We protect ourselves.
We avoid "the other."
Don't talk to strangers.
Yet, each acquaintance,
every friend,
even our best friend,
was once a stranger.
Strangers move
in and out of our lives.
Some quickly,
With intense impact.
Others linger,
Through the ebb and flow
Of a given moment.
Still others remain for the long haul.
No matter how long they stay,
or how intense the encounter,
each one-time stranger
has the potential
to change who we are.
Rather than avoid,
can we not welcome the stranger
and teach our children
the stranger may be an angel unaware,
and that we must listen to our truth,
learning to trust our intuition.

Exploration Studio 22: Uplift

Small waterfall with a rainbow outside Phoenix, Arizona

Find Your Voice

VENT.

If a heating system does not vent properly, dangerous fumes build up and cause harm. It's as simple as that: if we don't learn how to vent, we will eventually explode.

WE have the choice to announce, to babble, to grumble, to roar, to scream and shout, to whisper.

WE have the power to release the toxins building up in our psyche and our soul.

WE have the opportunity to vent before we explode and do damage to those around us.

Be Well

VITIATE.

To vitiate is to "spoil or impair the quality or efficiency" of something.

I think of how we often treat our bodies, minds, and spirits. We impair the quality of our lives, our relationships, and ourselves.

Body:

What habits do you have that might be spoiling the quality and efficiency of your body? Do you engage in too little or too much of anything?

Mind:

How do you ensure that your mind is nurtured? What are you doing today that will retain the quality of your mind?

Spirit:

Are you in a toxic situation? Do you operate on high alert in a constant state of fight, flight, or freeze? Is your current reality vitiating your soul?

Don't vitiate!

Choose Joy

Some days JOY is a gift. Other days it's an all-out BATTLE.

Unknown

Yes, we can choose to be joyful. We appreciate the beauty that surrounds us. We are grateful for all our blessings.

Somedays. We smile bravely amid struggles.

Somedays we do all these same things and do not FEEL joy. What then? I forge ahead—complete chores, get my body moving, eat well.

On days when JOY doesn't overwhelm us, we press on with confidence that JOY, like the sun on a cloudy day, is with us. We just can't feel it.

That feels a bit cliché, but JOY is more than a feeling. Joy is an attitude, a state of being rooted in hope, an acceptance of the dreary realities of life.

Move with Music

Secrets

Mary Lambert

Challenge Your Perspective

What are you ignoring?

忽視

neglect 忽 look at 視
without 勿 heart 心 spirit 礻 look 见

Walking from bed to bed in the children's ward of the government hospital on Christmas Eve, I watched as big brown eyes lit up at the sight of Santa hats, candy canes, and jingle bells. As we gathered in the nursery, I approached the infant lying in the first bed.

"What's his name?" I asked the attendee. "He has no name. He's just waiting to die." Her voice, matter-of-factly, held no compassion. She wouldn't even look at him.

Pulling back the covers to lift him, I saw the severe deformities: internal organs extending from his abdomen, no legs and only the stub of his left arm. His skull was deformed, and he had a cleft palate. I lifted him gently in my arms and, in a whisper, sang, "O come let us adore him" in the small child's ear. I wondered if my tears were for him or for his mother. I tried not to pass judgment, to offer peace instead of pity.

The Chinese words for *ignore* contain the radicals for *heart* 心 and *spirit* 礻. To ignore is to not look at something with your spirit and your heart. To ignore is to purposely choose not to engage the heart and spirit, to refuse to encounter the soul of another.

As a society, we house children in group homes and foster care. We drive by the homeless living in our viaducts. We grow complacent in addressing the needs of others—the poor, the mentally ill, the abandoned. When we ignore, we reject. Instead, we must choose how we will respond to the poor and homeless, to the one who has inflicted pain. We must choose not to ignore but to engage and, therefore, be transformed by the moment.

How we react to pain determines our character. How we acknowledge, embrace, and encounter the pain and hurt of another will, in turn, impact theirs.

But we don't only ignore others. We often ignore ourselves.

After I left the convent, someone asked me when I started to realize I needed to leave. My response: about five days in.

I know I'm not alone. How many of us stay in the wrong jobs, friendships, and marriages long after our hearts and souls nudge us to move on? How often do we stay stuck in our ways when our habits and patterns no longer serve us? Do we look with our hearts at the talent, the goodness, the bravery, and the greatness within ourselves? Or do we ignore it? Yes, it feels horrible to be ignored by someone we respect and love, but how often do we neglect to SEE with our hearts and our spirits what lies within us.

Ponder Poetry

Drip

3.2015

I felt it
the life drain out of my soul
like final waterdrops from the showerhead.
Drip, drip.
I was determined
to never work for the church again,
so here I sat
last line of an online resume declaring
I now want to be a Benefits Advisor,
USAJobs.gov.
Drip. Drip.
Hit submit.
Plop.

30 years gone.
The me I was could be no more.
With every ounce of hope I could muster
I claim I want THIS job
Because I could never again, ever,
seek employment in the church
the very organization, the community
that raised me,
shaped every fiber of my being
for whom I lived, moved, and had my being
the God, the Jesus, the Christ
they represented
I've said it before and always returned
Glutton for punishment
or victim of abuse
finding comfort with the abuser
believing if I only work harder,
do more, give more, be good
then, then they will see
that I am worthy.

My therapist. She says
I have issues with female authority.
What the hell?
I say I have issues with stupidity.
She says I need a boss I can respect

I say I need a boss that isn't stupid
They must feel threatened,
But I can't stop being me.
How about they have issues with me!
What did I do wrong?
Except dedicate every ounce—
my life's blood, sweat, and tears
to do my job
beyond everyone else's ability.
Never saying
"it's not in my job description."
But then when you believe
you are called to save the world
everything is in your job description.

Crying is a sign of weakness
But Jesus cried.
Crying shows a lack of faith
But Jesus cried.
Crying is unacceptable
But Jesus cried.

I am done saving the world
or righting the wrong or fighting the fight
And so, my soul inside will lie dormant
waiting, just waiting for that next step,
the door everyone promises will open,
the better things ahead,
the lessons learned and new adventures
the moment once again
when everything will be alright
Until that day
a day that may never come
because God loves the homeless,
the helpless, the deranged
as much as God loves anyone else
Until that day I push ahead
Not one day or hour or moment
But one iota in time
Drip, drip, plop

124

Exploration Studio 23: Wonder

First strawberries of the season

Find Your Voice

WHISPER.

A vague memory I hold from childhood is of an adult often saying, "Whispering is rude. If you can't share with everyone, don't share with anyone." Yet we were taught to whisper in churches, libraries, and even banks. I understand whispering in church and libraries, so we don't disturb those who are praying or reading. But banks?

The bank whisper first struck me at a bank in Hong Kong, where people shouted and raised their hands in the air. I was struck by the contrast to the almost churchlike atmosphere of the modern American bank where we stand in straight lines silently waiting for our turn to approach the teller. We've developed a reverence and serious sense of secrecy around money that cripples so many of us.

Only recently have we begun to speak openly about the atrocity of nonliving wages, full-time workers eating at soup kitchens, and the inequity of gender and race pay gaps. The person in need of a financial boost when they hit hard times is viewed as less than, a failure, or even criminal. Not to mention the secrecy and victim-shaming surrounding pedophilia, harassment, rape, domestic violence, and police brutality. Through whisper and secrecy, money gained the power to own, divide, and destroy individuals, families, and communities.

The cries for justice, equality, and equity for the oppressed and marginalized that turn into movements of change often begin with a whisper to a friend or even to a stranger.

Maybe you can't share with everyone, but please share with someone. Please stop keeping secrets that harm you. At the very least, whisper.

Be Well

WAKE UP.

The term "woke" has gained popularity in recent years in reference to people who try to be socially, and in particular racially, conscious.

Some folks embrace the word to describe themselves—proudly and boldly. Others use the word derogatorily to dismiss those who are fighting for justice.

I simply ask: Are you awake? Or do you need to wake up?

This "woke-ness" could be personal, interpersonal, social, professional, or political. You might be fully awake in one area of your life but not in another.

Do you travel through life as if you're sleepwalking? Do you simply allow life to happen to you and around you? What are you avoiding by not waking up?

Body:

Practically speaking, do you get enough sleep? Do you rely on caffeine or some other stimulant to stay awake? If you have a professional goal, do you move to make it happen? If you are made aware of an injustice, do you mobilize?

Mind:

Do you pay heed to the "little voice inside your head" and the "red flags" that warn you of impending danger? Do you trust the old tapes that keep you stuck, or do you listen to positive, motivating messages? Are you narrow-minded or do you look for new ways to understand and appreciate the world around you?

Do you acknowledge the many social issues (misogyny, racism, ableism, neurotypical standards, homophobia, and hetero-normative frameworks) that impede the potential for happiness, goodness and greatness in those who are excluded or oppressed?

Spirit:

Do you recognize and embrace the spirit moving in and out and throughout your life?

Are you awake to your own limitations? Are you aware of your own greatness? Are you moved by the pain and suffering of others?

Perhaps today is a good day to listen to **Wake Up Everybody.**

Choose Joy

Joy is what happens to us when we allow ourselves to recognize how good things really are.

Marianne Williamson

My favorite part of this quote is the phrase "what happens to us" because joy is more than a feeling. Rather, it is a state of being that envelops us when we look for the good in life.

We often spend our lives chasing success, wealth, and happiness. But if we breathe a simple "gratitude" into the present moment, joy arrives like a gift at the door.

Move with Music
Strong Enough

Des'ree

Challenge Your Perspective

Are you wise?

智

knowledge 知 day 日

I was raised with the biblical story of Solomon offering to split a baby in two in order to give half to each woman who claimed to be the mother. Somehow Solomon knew that the true mother would rather lose her baby to the care of another than have it killed. From this story, I carried the notion that wisdom required an ability to make a split-second decision.

While sometimes this is true, I profoundly appreciate the Chinese word for *wisdom*, which is comprised of *knowledge* 知 and *day* 日.

I could think of it in two ways:

- Wisdom is having the knowledge needed for the day.
- Wisdom is gained by collecting the knowledge from every day.

I began to understand that wisdom often comes with age and experience. Wisdom isn't just bestowed in an instant out of nowhere. Sure, sometimes we might feel like an answer or solution came to us out of the blue. I am often surprised by what comes out of my mouth while supporting someone struggling with a problem.

But if we dig deep, we can often find that a previous experience, something we've read, a word spoken by another in our own moment of need—led to the wisdom we've gained and our opportunity to share with others.

Wisdom isn't something that we automatically acquire when we hit a certain age or join a religious group. Wisdom is not stored in some hidden compartment waiting for a momentous occasion to manifest itself. Rather, wisdom is learning to tap into the knowledge given us as we survive each day.

When we take the time to truly listen, when we hear with our hearts, and when we reflect on our experiences in a spirit of gratitude, the lessons we encounter lead us to wisdom.

Wisdom is knowing what to say to my daughter when her best friend turns against her, to my son after he strikes out to lose the championship game, or to my spouse or best friend who struggles with a difficult boss.

Wisdom guides our daily decisions, gathering graces day-by-day to deal with life when we, or someone we love, faces illness, struggles with alcoholism or addiction, is going through a divorce or job loss, or living with grief. Wisdom is knowing when to rub an ear, hold a hand, wipe a tear or say good-bye.

Ponder Poetry

A Vision

I have no dream, as dreams are for sleep.
Instead, driven by passion
I hold a vision
A vision of children
rushing to school each morning
not because rule of law,
the best college, a job, a salary,
But a vision of children
Rushing into buildings of passion,
in communities of inspiration
where others ask not: what will you do when you grow up?
But who are you?
What do you wonder? What do you hope?
What do you desire?
A vision of children
Who thirst for learning, curiosity not yet shattered
By hours of rules and lectures and tests,
who have learned how to pick a or b or c
but long to discover the why, the how, the what
not circle a letter from a list.
A vision of children working together
To dream and envision and create
A neighborhood, a city, a world
where every child plays outside,
jumps rope on the sidewalk, and dreams of a future
because each child has a choice.
A vision of children who as toddlers
Filled with curiosity asked why
And still at thirteen ask, not in defiance
But from a single-hearted pursuit
to understand, to know,
to create possibility from problems,
solving puzzles and
bringing a new vision to reality.

Exploration Studio 24: Harmonize

Small indoor bamboo plant

Find Your Voice

XERISCAPE.

If you live in a xeric (arid) area, you'll have to xeriscape your garden. To xeriscape is "to reduce or eliminate the need for irrigation."

The idea of xeriscaping brought up a particularly tough period in my professional life. I was the newly hired head of a small private high school that had celebrated being debt-free just before my hire. Within 6 weeks of my arrival. I identified and had to manage a $1.2 million deficit. Handling the financial crisis while keeping morale up proved to be difficult.

For the life of me, I struggled to keep a small bamboo plant that someone gave me alive. At a faculty meeting, I placed the glass bowl filled with rocks that once had held the robust plant in the center of the room and shared my horticultural failure. I distributed the rocks and encouraged everyone, as they returned the rocks to the bowl, to privately acknowledge the "rocks" that weighed them down—their fear, discouragement, and frustration. I filled the bowl with water, symbolically washing away the negative feelings to encourage a fresh, clean start.

When all seems lost and we are feeling isolated and alone, we must xeriscape our lives. We must create an environment that supports our needs and doesn't require too much from us at the moment. We must find those tricks, hobbies, habits, activities, or people that offer a touch of beauty and a bit of joy, that give us strength and help us persevere through the dry, dark night of the soul.

The next morning when I arrived at my office, someone had replaced the bamboo plant and added a small note that read, "...sometimes we need to just water rocks...."

Be Well

XENOGRAFT.

To xenograft is "to obtain from a member of one species and transplant it to a member of another species."

The prefix "xeno-" means foreign. It comes from the Greek word *xenos*, meaning stranger, guest, or host.

What does this have to do with self-care and being well?

Xenograft is a medical term that focuses on grafting tissue from one part of the body to another.

I suggest that we consider "xenografting" more figuratively.

What can we do to introduce new and "foreign" activities or ideas into our lives?

Body:

Have you ever picked up a food you've never eaten and tried it? Do you shy away from trying new activities or forms of exercise?

Mind:

Do you try to learn about different cultural customs or languages? Do you ever read or have thought-provoking conversations about someone else's political beliefs? Have you let an earlier unpleasant experience of a topic or subject keep you from trying again?

Spirit:

Do you accept the traditions and beliefs passed onto you without question? Does questioning your beliefs frighten you? Have you questioned and embraced the answers as your own? Have you ever visited a church, temple, or place of worship of another religious tradition? Have you ever practiced a ritual from another spiritual practice?

Perhaps we don't want to make them our own, but is it so horrible to understand or experience that which is "foreign" or seems like another species altogether? Do we not stand to gain something by doing so?

Choose Joy

It is the broken road with pitfalls and sharp turns and unexpected traverses that has brought me joy and adventure.

Alice Walker

As our journey through life takes us through twists and turns, starts and stops, we are often faced with the question, "What's next?"

Perhaps before we ask, "What's next?" we might spend some time in review of our broken road. As we reflect—particularly on the moments of pain, the pitfalls and sharp turns— hindsight can bring new awareness of the positives that came from the negative.

The work I do today, which I thoroughly enjoy and am quite good at, would have never been possible without what I fondly refer to as my "Five Years of Failure" (2010-2015). During that time, I had three jobs where, in hindsight, I realize I made many decisions rooted more in fear than in acting proactively from a position of confidence and strength.

By embracing and owning my part in the pitfalls of those five years, I can let go of regret. And in letting go of regret, I can utilize the skills and experiences I gathered to offer much more to my clients.

On my broken road, I found joy.

You can, too.

Move with Music

What I Am

Cathy Richardson

Challenge Your Perspective

Are you anxious?

焦慮

scorched 焦 tiger 虍 think 思

When I say or think of the word *anxious* or *anxiety*, my body tenses.

The Chinese word for *anxiety* is made of the word for *scorched* 焦 (which is composed of the words for *bird* and *fire*) and a word that is created by a *tiger* 虍 over *think* or *ponder* 思 (which is made up of *brain* and *heart*).

A burning bird and a scorched tiger (or even a not scorched tiger).... Wouldn't these cause anxiety in anyone?

I never considered myself an anxious person, but about a decade ago when we were faced with an incredibly challenging financial situation, I lived in an almost constant state of anxiety and experienced frequent panic attacks.

Thankfully, those times have passed, but the lessons I learned remain. *(Note: If you are experiencing serious anxiety, please visit a health care professional. My thoughts are not meant to replace the advice of licensed professionals).*

The truth is, we are not likely to meet a burning bird or a tiger up close and personal any time soon. But when we allow ourselves to even ponder the possibility, we are right to worry.

The trick is to NOT focus on that which is not likely to happen.

I don't know too many people who are anxious because of birds and tigers. We are, however, anxious about unknown outcomes. Our anxiety is rooted in the possibility that something bad might happen or that we might fail.

And so, we ponder the burning birds and tigers—and we flee, freeze, or prepare to fight.

Instead, when we begin to feel anxious, and our minds wander into all that could possibly go wrong, perhaps we can replace the images conjured by burning birds and tigers with something more pleasant. Perhaps a few of our favorite things...

One of my personal favorites is daffodils. What would be your favorite? Which images can you invite into your thought processes when you begin to feel anxious? Kitty cats and puppies? Brownies and hot cocoa? Babies and cozy blankets?

In the process of visualizing things that bring comfort, peace, and joy, the scorching tigers fade.

Ponder Poetry

Depression

Chicago, 6.2015

Depression. Ashamed. Embarrassed.
Misunderstood.
Depression destroys lives.
Thrives on Secrecy.
Lives in Fear.
Fosters misunderstanding.
Depression feels heavy
Like the weight
One thousand pebbles
Sifting through my soul.
Robbing me of joy, hope, peace.
Pressing.
Pressing down.
Suffocating,
Stealing my voice.
Making me feel
Small.
Unworthy.
Broken.
Depression—anger turned inward.
Allowing the
Mean, Nasty, Evil
That exists in the world
To invade my soul.
Not on purpose.
Not because I lack will.
Because I care
Perhaps too much.

Exploration Studio 25: Magnify

Chicago skyline from North Ave

Find Your Voice

YES.

Shonda Rhimes, well-known writer, producer, and director of popular televisions shows like *Grey's Anatomy* and *Scandal* gave a TED Talk in 2016 that began, "So a while ago, I tried an experiment. For one year, I would say 'yes' to all the things that scared me. Anything that made me nervous, took me out of my comfort zone, I forced myself to say yes to."

To find our voice and be well, to find our radical heart, "Just YES it." Own YES as a verb, a call to action, a way of being.

As Shonda did, say YES to that which scares you, makes you nervous, and takes you out of your comfort zone.

Not sure you can accomplish something? YES it anyway. Envision success! YES in how you walk, the food you eat, the clothes you wear. YES life!

To YES life is to be BRAVE.

Be Well

YIELD.

To yield is to "produce or provide" or to "give way to."

Body:

I often think of yielding to the limitations of my body as I age. I cannot do what I used to do, and that's okay. But I also know that when I offer my body the best nutrients and sleep and exercise, my body yields fruit—more energy and action and more ability to continue to gift the world in some small way.

Mind:

What do you feed your mind, and what does it produce for you, your family, and the world? Do you consume news, entertainment, and content that yields a positive, hopeful, motivating mindset?

Do you need to "give way" to an idea or concept you've been resisting?

Do you need to "give way" to another in an argument?

Spirit:

Have you cultivated the soil of your soul to invigorate your spirit?

Do you "give way" to the promptings of the spirit? Do you allow the spirit to move you?

Choose Joy

Take risks for joy. Sometimes just saying yes can set your whole life into motion.

Unknown

Shonda Rhimes also wrote *Year of Yes*, a book written in conjunction with her TED talk.

In it, she shares how making the decision to say "yes" for one year to anything that frightened or challenged her personally and professionally not only changed her life but saved it.

In a witty and sometimes laugh-out-loud-funny way, she covers important topics about insecurity, playfulness, fear, love, courage, friendship, feminism, motherhood, weight—the list goes on and I am doing a disservice by even trying to explain it. If you haven't read it, I recommend you do.

Shonda's *Year of Yes* is all about taking risks that ultimately lead to unexpected joy.

While my "risk" and your "yes" may never lead us to lunch with Oprah or fancy awards ceremonies like Shonda's, I'm willing to bet it will lead to unexpected places, and unexpected joys.

Move with Music
I Ain't Movin'

Des'ree

137

Challenge Your Perspective

Are you humble?

恭順

respectful 恭 arrange 順

The Chinese expression for *humility* comes from the character for *respectful* 恭 placed next to the character for *arrange* 順.

To respectfully arrange.

If we have natural talent, if we have struggled to acquire knowledge and skill, if we happened upon some blessing of beauty, wealth, or personality, humility does not demand that we hide or be embarrassed.

On the contrary, humility requires that we acknowledge our strengths and blessings. Humility also dictates that we acknowledge the strengths and gifts of others.

Life is not a competition. Life is complementation. Through the proper ordering of all we are given, as individuals and as a society, we keep things in perspective. The gift of one complements and completes the gift of another.

Humility then does not mean putting ourselves down or hiding our talents but rather recognizing that we are a small part of a much bigger picture.

Humility does not mean pretending we are not very good at something, but when we are humble, we acknowledge and appreciate when others are better. We don't always have to be the best. And even if we are better at one skill or tasks than another, that doesn't make us a better person.

Humility is remembering that we are no more than we are in the sight of God—*and no less.*

Ponder Poetry

Non-Resignation

Chicago, 2.16.2015

I will not resign
Myself to a world of mediocrity.
Instead, I will
Step forward
One foot
One moment
In grace
Into a
World of possibility.
Accept this as
My letter
Of non-resignation.
Not resigned
To days spent in
Nonsensical recall
of inane material
That has no hold on me.
No use for the future.
Useless Information
Not education.
No challenge
No way to stop the hate
Drive the peace
Overcome the injustice.
Receive my non-resignation to
Why those of darker skin
And rougher hands
Remain outcast
And downtrodden
Or should I say trodden upon?
Cast out
And kept down.
I will not resign.

Not until
The hours of a child's day
Are filled with wonder
And challenge
And meaning.
Not until
Every child is
Presented the tools
and the opportunity
To change their world.
I will not resign
Until my letter Is the letter
That does not rest on the backs
of poor children
But is posted
Boldly. Proudly. Defiantly.
Like the letters of two Luthers
For all to read.
A letter of non-resignation
Calling out those
who should know better.
Those who claim
a higher call.
Those who hold the futures
of our next generation
in the power of their pens.
The power of the yay or nay.
The power of the schedules
and rules and regulations that
form our next generation.
Accept my letter of non-resignation
to the status quo.

Exploration Studio 26: Flourish

Moonshot

Find Your Voice

ZOOM IN.

To really find our voice and own our truth, we need to zoom in on what is truly important. Trying to speak up at every moment and fight every battle can get exhausting.

We cannot accomplish everything at once. Being true to ourselves and claiming our voice will take practice, trial and error, and persistence.

We might find ourselves lashing out at others, pointing fingers, being harsh.

We might realize that choices we made long ago have trapped us in boxes or behind bars, making it difficult to break free.

We might discover that we only have the energy to babble, grumble, or whisper when all we want to do is scream. We have not yet found the courage.

By deciding to ZOOM IN on one technique or one action or one aspect of finding our voice, until we are confident that we have accomplished that goal, we will have the energy to move on to the next one.

By staying focused on practical steps to VOICE our truth, we will maintain the physical and psychic energy we need to face the messiness that might come from the struggle.

Finding your voice and owning your truth is not a one and done. Each phase in life greets you with new opportunities to speak up, speak out, and speak for yourself and others.

Be Well

ZINC.

As a verb, *zinc* means, "to treat or coat with zinc; to galvanize."

In handling my light-skin tendency toward pre-cancer conditions, I've learned that zinc is the best option for sunscreen. I now galvanize my face each morning to protect it from sun damage.

But we also can consider how we *zinc* our bodies, thoughts, and emotions. What helps to *zinc* you from that which could cause rust and corrosion?

Body:

- Exercise
- Sleep
- A good walk, run or bike ride

Mind:

- Repeating positive affirmations
- Engaging in a relaxing hobby
- Smashing things
- A good stiff drink

Spirit:

- Meditation
- Coffee or tea with a friend
- Cuddling with a loved one
- Sitting on the beach

Choose Joy

Make joy your compass today.

Unknown

A magnetized compass offers direction in relation to true north. It is NOT a map or a set of instructions on how to get where you are going.

A geometrical compass measures distance between points and draws circles and arcs from a specific center.

From this perspective, if we allow joy to be our compass, it can either point us in the direction we want to go (follow your heart's desire, your true north) or redirect us if we are lost. Or it can help us recognize the boundaries within which we are called to find joy (be still and accept the moment, bloom where you are planted).

Like physical compass instruments, metaphorical compasses each serve a different purpose.

Sometimes we are meant to find joy in the given moment and circumstances within our reach (geometrical), but at other times we are led on an adventure driven by a yearning for possibility (magnetic).

We may savor life within the circumference of our authentic selves, or we may be called on a journey to seek our true north.

Either way, the compass reminds us that we will only find joy in relation to our authentic selves.

Move with Music
Try Everything
Shakira

Challenge Your Perspective

Are you hopeful?

望

dead (broken sickle) 亡 moon 月 earth 土

One of the Chinese characters for *hope* is the pictorial representation of a person with a broken sickle gazing at the moon.

Imagine being a farmer with your only instrument: a sickle. When that sickle breaks, your livelihood is destroyed. What can you do but gaze at the moon?

Have you ever felt a sense of hopelessness?

We throw our hands in the air, drop to our knees, put our head in our hands, and weep. As if we're admitting and inviting defeat.

But this image of a person standing tall on the earth, broken sickle in hand, gazing at the moon has a completely different energy.

I'm reminded of the superhero stance. Have you ever tried standing feet apart, fists on your hips, chest out, chin up, eyes ahead? The very act itself can be empowering.

To hope is to move beyond what is right in front of us to what lies ahead.

The Lutheran theologian Søren Kierkegaard said, "Hope is a passion for the possible."

What if, instead of sulking when we are disappointed and things seem hopeless, we zoom in on the desire of our hearts, zinc our thoughts and emotions, set our compass to find our true north, and take the first step forward?

Let's embrace a passion for all that is possible!

Ponder Poetry

Hope

For what do you hope?

Sunshine on a rainy day.
A sports team victory.
A sale on your favorite shoes.
Simple, everyday pleasures.
Trivial. Meaningless. Wishing.

Food on the table.
A roof overhead. A good job.
Financial stability. Health.
Fundamental rights.
Reasonable. Practical. Sensible.

To love and be loved.
Life. Liberty. Happiness.
Our own well-being.
Desires of the soul.

In what or whom do you hope?

Money. Politics. Medicine. Religion.
The Universe. A higher power. Your God.
Your family. Your friends. Yourself.

For what do you hope?
In what or whom do you hope?

How long will you hope?

NEXT UP? Stay Grounded

Redwoods near Lake Tahoe, California

Next Up: Stay Grounded

As we come to the end of the Exploration Studios, I invite you to ponder the California redwood tree.

Growing up in northern California, I was unaware of how fortunate I was to live near the California redwoods. If you've never experienced standing at the foot of a giant redwood tree, please put it on your bucket list. If you can, visit Muir Woods near San Francisco, Henry Cowell Park near Santa Cruz, or Humboldt County in northern California.

I hope one day you have an opportunity to experience the beauty, majesty, and strength of the redwood that I finally learned to appreciate as a young adult.

The size and age alone are breathtaking. The average height is about 200 to 250 feet—some reaching heights in the 300s. They average 10 to 15 ft in diameter, with some as much as 40 ft around. And they live between 1000 and 2000 years!

But the most remarkable aspect of these spectacular creatures is their roots.

The redwood has no permanent tap root—the long root which grows deep into the ground, anchoring many bushes and trees.

Instead, the roots of a redwood grow outward, spreading shallowly as they twist, turn, and secure themselves around the roots of their neighbors. Their power, strength, and sturdiness come, not from being solitary, but because of their interdependence on nearby trees.

The redwood stands strong because of its community.

Now that you've taken the time to *get rooted* through radical _personal_ exploration, I encourage you to learn from the redwood. Find others to continue exploring with you. Surround yourself with a community that embraces you and helps you *stay grounded.*

Exploring together will open new avenues, offer new insights, and empower you so that like the majestic, magnificent redwood, you will THRIVE.

About the Get Rooted, Stay Grounded & Thrive Companion Journal

The Companion Journal to *Get Rooted, Stay Grounded & Thrive* is designed as a safe and sacred space to capture your feelings, thoughts, and expressions on your journey. You will find prompts for further personal exploration and questions to spark community conversations.

About the Author

Janet Cobb is an author, speaker, and professional and personal development coach. She integrates her experience of starting over personally and professionally, more than once, with lessons learned as a former Catholic nun, teacher, fundraiser, school administrator, and current wife and mother of three young adult children, to offer encouraging accountability to women as they envision and create the life they desire.

Janet's previous publications include a children's nonfiction book written with her eight-year-old daughter Janalie, titled, *Raising Butterflies: to set them free;* a memoir of her thirteen years in the convent titled, *Surviving Sanctity: One Woman's Journey from Welfare, to Religion, to Sanity;* and a business book titled, *Promised Land: The 10 Commandments for Nonprofit Strategy, Communications, and Fundraising.*

You can find Janet at **www.janetcobbcoaching.com**.